FORTNIGHT AT BERNIE'S

An Aussie's 2020 Bernie Journey

Greg Dawson

I'd like to thank Bolly, Barney, Gerry, Jakob, Matt, and my mum. Their outstanding guidance, feedback, and support was essential in pulling this little tale together.

I dedicate this to the champions of progressivism found both in this book and all around the world. May their tireless efforts bring about a healthier, safer, and kinder world.

Contents

PART 1
Countdown to the Iowa Caucuses

1.

IC minus 3: Cops Arresting Junkies in Starbucks

My wife understood. She gave up on her faint protestations halfway through her first sentence after I verbalised my plans. So I arrived at O'Hare International 3 days before the 2020 Iowa Caucuses to volunteer with Bernie Sanders' presidential campaign.

Looks on people's faces ranged from curious to flabbergasted when asking why I cared enough, as an Aussie who lives and works in Korea, to trudge through knee-deep snow on American lawns and perch myself on icy steps (risking outrageous US hospital bills, as I was well aware) just to get told that Bernie's too old and a wacky socialist anyway. And yet, there I was. Why?

My well-practised answer comes in:

- a brief 15-20 second snapshot (the most socially acceptable),
- a 3 to 5-minute summary,

\- or the people-awkwardly-looking-at-their-watch version, which I try (with varying degrees of success) to only wheel out when there is accompanying food and/or drink, i.e. grab a couple of cases of beer and strap yourself in for a long weekend of endless rants.

I almost always internalised my simultaneous sense of surprise when people exclaimed,

'Wow! You've come all the way over here to Bumfucksville! But you're not even 'Murican!'

People who hang on to the delusion that what the US gets up to (mischievous little critters) doesn't have an outrageous influence on people all over the world, just haven't thought it through. Or they've never left their Americentric existence spent exclusively on US soil. I've heard it suggested that the whole world should be able to vote in US Presidential elections – if only that were true!

In the interests of keeping the show rolling, I'll restrain myself to a little snapshot answer. For now.

Why here? Why now? Why Bernie?

1. Global leadership on aggressively addressing climate change.
2. Scaling back destructive military interventionism (and exploitative trade deals).
3. Setting a guiding example of how representative democracy should truly work in the genuine best interests of the vast majority of people.

The rest of the Democratic field have, with varying degrees of lip-synching commitment, started singing from the same songbook. But Bernie has a 40-year record of banging out the same tunes, even when the crowd was almost empty. And even with the recently increased popularity of his catchy melodies, he has not sold out to the lures of corporate riches: signed no big-label record deals, enlisted no flashy marketing managers or self-interested promoters looking to get him to compromise his artistic integrity to raise their cut.

Same songs. Same complete lack of any attempt at false harmonising; just quality lyrics. A Dylan of the political world, perhaps.

For a pertinent actualisation of this ambitious analogy, may I present to you Bernie, the world's least melodious folk singer, making no attempt whatsoever to sing Woody Guthrie's 'This Land is Your Land' (and other tunes), when invited to contribute to a 1987 folk album as Mayor of Burlington, Vermont. He just uses his distinctive Jewish Brooklynite drawl to speak his way undeterred through the lyrics. Excruciatingly bad, and yet so charming (maybe I'm a little biased here).

YouTube: Flashback: Bernie Sanders' 1987 Folk Album

No pretenses. Zero bullshit.

I strode excitedly through the glistening corridors of O'Hare, was forced to buy something I didn't want (the first of way too many shitty food choices on this trip) to get change to put into one of the lifeless rows of exact-change-only machines in the attendantless train station entrance. Locals were effortlessly kind & helpful in pointing me in the right direction.

Wandering the streets as I closed in on my hotel in Chinatown, I felt that vague sense of self-concern for the first time in many years. The walk was through one of those well-past-its-heyday, semi-industrial areas (that has so far escaped gentrification) just on the outskirts of downtown, that you find in many large cities. The shiny airport and city centre quickly dropped off into run-down, real America, as I believe is the oft-used term these days for anything not glowing with affluence. I nervously dragged my luggage through the shabby, almost deserted streets to the hotel I'd booked, less than a kilometre from the 'Bernie Bus' that I'd be jumping on early the next morning to transplant me to Iowa.

The hotel was nice, for one of the cheapest ones I could find online in that area, and I hunkered down in my room, looking out at the Friday night lights beaming out from downtown Chicago. Another time, I would have swung in to check it all out, but I quickly decided not to. I wanted to be fresh in the morning.

I was peckish, though, and went into the Starbucks that adjoined the hotel to make the next in my cavalcade of appalling food choices that fattened me up about a kilogram a week on this trip, despite trudging around for hours on end every single day. Grabbed a ham and egg roll that was dripping with cheese, and a muffin. Dinner of champions.

Snacking on my bad decisions, I noticed an unnecessary number of big, well-armed cops hassling a couple of skinny, dishevelled dudes not far from my regret, as 2 enormous police wagons (everything's big) silently flashed their lights outside.

Cops arresting junkies in Starbucks! I'd arrived.

You don't have to wander too far off the tourist path to realise that the smiling face of America quickly cracks and sometimes looks in need of more than just heavy make-up to mask it - it needs a facelift or, to be honest, some serious reconstructive surgery.

I wasn't interested in rubbernecking, so I slunk back into my hotel room and crashed early.

A. Mini-rant 1 – The System is Diseased

The conditions that brought us Trump were 40 years of neoliberal privatisation, deregulation, slashing of trade unions, and gutting supportive public infrastructure, while at the same time gaming the system to favour the mega-wealthy, who were the ones absurdly receiving tax cuts, bailouts, and endless government benefits,

> *'Socialism for the rich, and rugged individualism for the poor', as MLK so poignantly observed in 1968.*

Even though not having to hear Trump's idiotic, bigoted, reckless, repugnant claptrap would soothe the offended sensibilities of people sitting in affluent living rooms, it would not remove the underlying dissatisfaction for so many that created the fertile conditions that allowed the rise of a tough-talking, scapegoating, faux-strongman like Trump. Merely going back to the same pre-Trump America would be like putting a band-aid on a gaping, festering predator-drone wound.

Despite depictions otherwise, Trump is not an aberration. He didn't just appear out of nowhere. Happy, successful, prosperous nations do not elect odious, self-absorbed, reprehensible bullies. Not having to listen to the orange-headed imbecile abuse everyone that doesn't feed his arrogance and need for endless false praise would indeed be a breath of fresh air, but toxic air from the existing system would remain and would continue to seep into your lungs, just a little more discreetly. Then down the track another, more organised, right-wing reactionary leader would be likely to rise up, and this time they could bring with them some actual intelligence and have structured plans to implement true authoritarian controls.

The US system has ravaged endless small towns, as well as urban and suburban communities, bringing about severe suffering through job losses to cheaper labor markets, depressed wages, a deficient health-care system, and part-time service industry jobs with unreliable hours and no benefits. These factors all cater to the booming and ever-increasing profits of fewer and fewer companies across the land as mega-companies like Walmart and Amazon swallow up small and middle-sized businesses with their relentless predatory pricing and resultant monopolisation.

This has brought about frustration, resentment, tension, and anger, leading to diseases of despair, such as the opioid epidemic devastating communities across the land, with suicide rates going up and average life expectancies going down for the first time in generations. Combine this with a myriad of other untended issues like broken infrastructure, e.g. poisoned water in many parts of the country, not just Flint, and rising racial tensions over disproportionate brutality shown by cops towards minorities, particularly black men, through a racist criminal justice system.

People have had enough. They have become ripe picking for vile, opportunistic right-wing media and politicians, working in loathsome unison, to scapegoat immigrants and minorities by pointing fingers at them for causing this pain. Fingers that should be pointed at the unrelenting greed of corporations who have no consideration for the health and well-being of people or the environment, just increased revenue for board members and stockholders.

A cure must be found. Trump is the symptom of a broken system, not the disease itself, and the way to remove Trump and banish him and his kind into the dustbin of history is by providing a genuine cure.

2.

IC minus 2: Bring Out your Hunched Shoulders and Bird-Nest Hair

Fresh and ready to go, I wandered down to reception at 5.15am and asked them if they could book a cab for me.

'A cab? Just use Uber.'

Ah, Korea had banned Uber, making me an Uber virgin (for want of a better expression).

'How long do you think it would take for a cab to come?'

'I'm not sure, sir. At this hour, maybe half an hour. Maybe more,' he said, holding his politeness while looking at me as though I was a luddite.

I should've downloaded Uber immediately and figured it out, but the bus was leaving at 6am and I didn't know how long it would take for an Uber to arrive, anyway (later learning that it would have been just a few minutes). So, being a dopey prick, I decided to shuffle down to the bus on foot, which was exactly what I'd planned to avoid.

It was still pitch black outside and it seemed like a pretty rough part of town. But it was only about 6 or 7 hundred metres and it was just off the road I was on; it would take a spectacularly poor effort to get lost. There should be some cars around in case there's a problem. How bad could it be? I was trying to rationalise away my lurking inner fears.

I barely remember seeing a single vehicle the whole walk, and the streets were lit by lights each about as bright as a candle. I walked past abandoned factories and under a couple of decent sized bridges; yep, the type that people sleep under. Shadowy figures lurched out of dark enclaves and a few eyeballs came my way; an ignorant, idiotic tourist just begging to be cracked over the head with a broken pipe and dragged into the corner of a disused factory, never to be discovered, as some previously down-on-his luck chap gets to parade around with a nice new collection of Bernie T-shirts. I was shitting myself, as I tried to figure out the acceptable speed to be going that was purposeful, but didn't look like panicky fleeing from every flickering glance of life. My heart was racing.

'Is this the Bernie Bus?'

'Yeah, jump on!'

'Great!', I said in a tone that I pretended was excitement, but was actually full-bodied relief.

We sped to Iowa across snowy plains, and along the way I took possibly the worst ever photo of crossing the mighty Mississippi into Iowa. I chatted with warm, engaging, funny, intelligent folks that were a perfect sample set of the multitude of similar people I loved hanging out with over the next 2 weeks. These were my people. A constantly rotating group I'd never seen before and with names often unlearnt. But I've never felt more at home.

The bus driver was a charismatic, entertaining Londoner. He delighted in revealing that he was a Trump voter (as a naturalised US citizen), which was met with jovial cheers, and led to continual good-hearted jibes in both directions,

'You'll be lucky to make it to Iowa.'

'Who knows how to drive a bus? Let's hijack this fucker,' which he loved.

Oh, the mirth. The mood was infectious - fun, but focused. Genuine camaraderie.

The London larrikin told us all how he thought ferrying a pile of badge-wearing Bernie freaks to Iowa would suck. But late in the trip he dropped his hard-man jokester guard a little and admitted to being completely misguided in his expectations and thought now that we were worthy of the utmost praise and admiration for being such a witty and enlightened group of trailblazers, fighting for greater justice for all and that we were quality company that should be sought out and cherished,

'Ah, you lot aren't actually that bad,' he muttered over the speaker system.

I had a 5-minute chat with him when we arrived (after excitedly following the crew straight into the branch office without my bigger bag - the only one put under). He had the thingy open and the bag was ready and waiting for my return. He puffed on a fag (as he would call it), and gave that cliched, confused spiel about how he liked Trump 'telling it how it is' - the first of countless times I heard this on my journey. Like many, he seemed unaware of how differing policies affected him, but just liked how his preferred candidates sounded, looked, or presented themselves. This comes as no great surprise, as US political media coverage has descended into a polarised celebrity popularity contest - by design - where style is presented as superior to substance.

He was a cracking lad - just pissed off with the whole political scene and saw Trump as the guy to break it all up.

'He talks like the rest of us, doesn't take shit, and is a breath of fresh air.'

His version of this recurring misconception continued and, as always, I listened attentively and agreed with many of his grievances, but not so much on the solutions.

He explained how he kinda liked Bernie, despite what they say - 'they', I presume, being Fox News, but could apply to just about any mainstream media. In my soon-to-be fairly considerable experience of speaking with regular punters across the full spectrum of political support, pretty much everybody did. When it came to appraising his character, at least. With one memorable exception at a knocked door in small town New Hampshire,

'Get the fuck off my lawn you fucking communists!'

We did. Both my canvassing partner and myself checking with heightened senses to see if he had a shotgun nearby. We couldn't see one, but there must have been one lurking not far off. Not near enough, though, thankfully.

This not-entirely-stable lad might just have had some unkind words about Bernie had we had the opportunity to engage in a lengthy, probing, and far-ranging discussion, but we didn't get too far past his opening gambit. Other than this notable exception, in my many hundreds of voter interactions, not a soul that I can remember ripped into Bernie as a person; plenty of forthright admissions that they had strong objections about his politics, but even those were often followed by rejoinders like 'But he seems like an honest guy who believes in what he says'. People smell integrity. Bernie has it in spades.

The branch office in Waterloo was teeming with life, bubbling with energy and enthusiasm. The majority was coming from kids in their 20s. Not entitled avocado-toast-eating brats, but rather a multi-racial group of smart youngsters who've figured out the best way to fight for a productive future for themselves. These were the group most impressed that I had made my way over there, far from my own, to join them.

'Thanks, man. That's awesome.'

Those that I gained an almost inexplicable affinity with were those who were closer to my age or above, almost all of whom nodded with immediate unspoken respect and understanding for my pilgrimage. Many of them had also left spouses to keep the home fires burning. These people had got on board not so much for themselves, most of whom seemed comfortable enough to be able to leave workplaces and hometowns to set about the task in Iowa that they were drawn to. Well-off enough to not need to fight for change for themselves, but emotionally invested enough to care about the plight of so many others, whose current condition or future prospects were not as bright. Not personal gain, but awareness, empathy, and an innate desire to get involved with what felt right.

'Not me, us!'

'Fight for someone you don't know!'

These campaign slogans were never truer than for these people. Clichés, sure, but perfect encapsulations of the motivations of this older brigade. I gravitated towards them, and uncovered comfort and connection within seconds.

After soaking up some positive vibes, a couple of rallying and instructional speeches, and more shitty food, a group of us volunteered to go out to another canvassing base about 20 minutes away, and I got a lift over with Rob and Brittany, a motivated young couple who'd trekked over (well, flown and rented a car) from San Francisco.

Great decision!

The local leftie rep, Chris Schwartz, the Black Hawk County Supervisor and LGBTQ activist, had an expansive mansion. The San Franciscans and I fuelled up on a lavish spread of hearty (but not healthy) delights that, like in every Bernie launching pad, were laid on. The encouragement to get your fill was warmly received by loyal foot soldiers either returning to base or preparing to head out to pound the pavement. We were allocated our canvassing code, which we entered into our - at least, my - recently downloaded MiniVAN app containing relevant voter info. As we prepared to head out, one of the code-wielders asked us, almost off-handedly,

> 'Would you guys be able to be back here before 3 because Nina Turner, Cornel West, and Susan Sarandon are coming here (pointing to the living room floor that we were standing on) to fire up the troops and thank everyone and we want a good turnout?'

'Ah, yeah, sure,' I said with false calmness, as I did my best not to also blurt out, 'You'd better fucking believe it. Wouldn't miss it for the world'.

For those of you that only recognise the name of the Academy Award winner amongst those three, she was the least cause of my excitement.

SNT, Senator Nina Turner, is a one-woman firebrand of political power, passion and persuasion. She is like a gospel minister reaching the crescendo of a particularly empowered sermon - turned up to 11 - using her boundless repertoire of voice, body, and soul to enliven pulsating and adrenaline-charged responses. And that's just when she's ordering a coffee. She ramps it right up to rapturous levels of dynamism when she's preaching the gospel of Bernie to an appreciative crowd.

If there's one person, in political realms, who can compete with her in her strongest categories, that'd be Dr. Cornel West. His ultra-charisma glows as he reels off his majestic blend of political poetry with his well-worked hip-hop rhymes flowing out in rapid rhythm without skipping a beat, all the while espousing complex political and philosophical background and seamlessly weaving it into a contemporary context. His wealth of knowledge, insight, and brilliant exposition has led him to share his great wisdom in such sketchy schools as Dartmouth, Princeton, Yale, Harvard, and Hull (the last one is not true, but is an homage to one of my favourite Blackadder jokes).

And Susan Sarandon.

She is wonderfully well-spoken and a gloriously kind-hearted moral crusader. But if you're looking for a gee up, she was out of her depth. I was full of anticipation and childlike excitement as we worked the quiet streets of outer Waterloo.

The 3pm arrivals lived up to everything I expected, which you may have just realised, was quite a lot. I was teary-eyed as I looked on from half-way up a stairwell, only metres away. They all spoke with characteristic vigour, passion, purpose, and love. I was pumped up.

We spilled out onto the vast front yard, following instructions for a group photo. In the post-photo mass of people, I was carefully dodging my way out of the congestion when I turned and about to bump into me was Dr. West,

'Ooooh, my brother. You're doing fine work, brother.'

He was working the crowd and seemed almost more excited than us, and we were all well fired up. Before I could say a word, he embraced me,

'Bring it in, my brother.'

I did.

Everyone was on a selfie rampage, so almost without realising, I jumped on board. Cornel magnanimously obliged post-hug - I think it was his idea. He has a huge presence, that is matched by his immense wisdom, intellect, kindness, and head – all enormous.

He seemed committed to hugging everyone there. As that euphoric melee continued, I spied Susan Sarandon, smiling at the Cornel love-fest as she stood by the car about to whisk them away to continue the show elsewhere. My pluck was up after my first ever celebrity selfie, so without stopping to think, I found myself in front of her, very politely requesting my second.

'Oh, sweetie. Of course.'

I couldn't have been happier. Off to a cracking start.

A few more doors then Angie and I met as planned and set off towards Cedar Rapids. As I would do on countless occasions, I had asked a campaign official if they knew of anyone heading to the Bernie event that evening (or a similar request). They shouted a quick room announcement - problem solved.

21

Angie and I shared a mini road trip for an hour or two, and hung out at a Bernie rally for three or four more, and we are friends for life. We're still trading WhatsApp messages to share joys and heartbreaks, or to let off steam to a fellow hyper-tuned-in follower of US political antics by launching into a curse-laden tirade about some godawful act against Bernie, or human decency. Top shelf solidarity. She is a champion of monumental proportions.

Up from Albuquerque (the setting for Breaking Bad, if you're looking for visualisation) and ripping in for the campaign. Sharp as a tack, super-organised, strongly focused on all the right things, and great company. She'd put up her hand to be a Precinct Captain at one of the remote caucus sites, and offered me a tiny glimpse of nerves, as she was about to become a first-time caucus goer and was so keen to do it to the utmost of her ability. It didn't take much firing her up with richly deserved praise, before she got on board,

'Shit, yeah. You're right. I'm gonna smash this out of the park.'

And she did. She later ran me through the rousing speech she gave and tactical nous she employed to win her caucus site for Bernie. She is one of the good'uns.

There was rock-concert buzz in the venue well before the speakers came out. Angie and I had settled in and continued chatting like old mates. We discovered that neither of us had seen Bernie in his wrinkly flesh before, and we were both kid-in-a-candy-store-the-day-before-Christmas excited. We regaled each other with stories about how and when we first had the epiphany that Bernie was the only prominent politician who actually stood with the people against the corporate stranglehold that both major political parties had perfected over our lifetimes,

'Follow the money. That's all you need to do, goddammit. It's simple. Bernie's the only one 100% people funded and thus free from corporate influences. He wants what's best for the overwhelming majority, not the tiny minority of ultra-wealthy and uber-powerful that dominate the political donor class and own most gigantic corporations, including fossil fuel industries, arms manufacturers, pharmaceutical giants, Wall St. financial empires, as well as the major media conglomerates that tell us who to support. Greedy, self-interested cocksuckers that have no interest in doing what's right, only what increases their obscene profits.'

'Yep, spot on. That's why it's no surprise that neither party has genuinely fought for aggressive action against global warming, reducing foreign conflicts, a universal public medical system (and control of drug prices), or the breakup of the very same banking behemoths that ruined the world economy in 2007/8 and got bailed out by the taxpayers, who were the ones that lost jobs and homes in their millions. All the while being told that the politicians they were conditioned to support were on their side because they advocate for the factionally accepted opinions (deemed correct by your 'side') concerning social and cultural issues, such as gay rights and abortion, which are extremely important, of course, but have limited effect on the bottom line for the economic and military titans that run the show. They manufacture opposing mobs to vehemently argue over these differences, while both parties roll on with favorable policies for the economic and military money-making machines owned and run by their oligarchic donors.'

'Absolutely. And what about...'

I have a solid group of mates in Seoul who share similar conversations. We don't live in a bubble, though, as we also have discussions with many people, most of whom also detest Trump and all things Republican but get on the backfoot if you also throw criticisms the way of the Democratic Party. Many people are so caught up in this media-driven, polarised, duo-political paradigm, where speaking ill of a Democratic representative, candidate, or policy can easily provoke a backlash accusation of being a Republican supporter or at least sympathiser, and vice-versa. Attacking both parties from a position representing the people's best interests often confuses people who want you to conform to their media-ordained requirement to pigeonhole you into picking a 'team'. Without any face-painting, or flag-waving, I prefer the disappointing Blue Donkeys to beat the more destructive Red Elephants, but when sharing my opinion that the Donkeys could get better players, tactics, and management, it can ruffle a few feathers.

Right now, though, my views were liberated in this auditorium packed with throngs of fervently like-minded people, and we were all abounding in the joy of bellowing out our beliefs at the top of our lungs. It was therapeutic and was giving me a warm, spirited glow from tip to toe. My tingling gut and eyes glazed with emotion would become a recurring sensation for me over the next fortnight, and the emotional charge from this evening stayed with me for many weeks to come. It was an unburdening of the soul, and not to put too much of a delicate point on it, I was fucking loving it.

I've said innumerable times over the last 4 or 5 years about how my love for Bernie is based on his policies. That's what captivates me. It's not a cult of personality thing. It's the message, not the man.

Right now, all of that was on hold.

Both pretty level-headed adults over 40, we were revelling in this chance to carry on like 14-year-olds waiting to see the leather-clad pop heartthrob that adorned every inch of their bedroom walls for the first time. Except the object of our dizzying devotion was a shouty grandfather from rural Vermont with no fashion sense whatsoever and hair that was resistant to both product and comb.

The exuberant atmosphere continued to allow us, no, encourage us, to verbalise this devotion by yelling out any sudden thought or emotion that seemed fit to add to the buoyant hubbub,

'C'mon, Bernster. Bring out your hunched shoulders and bird-nest hair and let's hear you give it some.'

Stuff like that - lost in the raucous cauldron of similar support.

I recalled a mate of mine, another Aussie called Greg, saying years before how cool it would be to get to a Bernie rally, and I now sent him a photo of my beaming dial as that dream had become reality. Pretty soon I'd send him a photo of the great man in action.

Michael Moore fired the crowd up with broadsides against the 'machine', interspersed with slightly strained obscenities to hammer home his points. Then the ever-delightful Jane Sanders spoke. Imagine if she were first lady. Life would be better. Then first Cornel followed by Nina both ignited a virtuous cycle of zest and fervour with the heaving adoration that surrounded them, as they carried on spitting fireballs of justice and love as though they never stop. We started feeling a bit jumpy and fidgety. We knew Bernie was coming out soon.

'There he is. Bernie fucking Sanders.'

The crowd went full on Beatlemania. I was jumping out of my skin with visceral, unbridled elation.

The big fella didn't disappoint. He rattled off his unvarnished playlist of angry-love hits. Critiquing the ills of the system AND proffering practical, achievable ways to correct them. It's the latter part in particular where his opponents show themselves to be lacking. What a good guy. He cares.

The crowd was pumped as Bernie struck his final chords of people-centric solutions and then, in one of my all-time favorite Bernie moments, he got to show the absurd confluence of events that made him an unlikely DJ introducing the musical act that will wrap up festivities. With the clunky style of your beer-lovin' uncle who has just woken up from a turkey-bloated Xmas afternoon nap and finds himself the confused host of a primetime radio show,

> 'Time now to boogie along to the instrumental beats and lyrical interludes of these talented young band members, whose rock will groove you all around the clock,' or some ungainly, dated equivalent that no doubt would've sounded far more apt on a wireless introducing Bing Crosby's latest chartbusters when Bernie was a boy.

Pure gold.

In my nerdy prep for this adventure, I even made a playlist for myself of Vampire Weekend songs, the groovers for the evening, and had been brushing up. I knew a couple of their songs already; I had the soft nostalgic lures of 'Step' stuck in my head for months after I first heard it a few years back and it kind of became my 'Bernie song' in 2015/6 (after listening to VW at a few rallies then, back when I was a mere online rally-goer). Their quirky and catchy 'Oxford Comma' was a bit of a fav, too. I really like them and not just 'cos they're part of the Bernie show, although that obviously helps. I got to know a pile more of their songs leading into tonight, and was lapping up the chance now to savour their show-reel selections. I came away with a new 'Bernie song' for this go-around: 'This Life'. It was up-beat and neatly captivated my mood at the time; uplifting in tone, but contrasted with an underlying sense of concern. Wonder if Bernie found it groovy.

B. Mini-rant 2 – Trump is the Symptom

Trump pounced on the chance to vocalise the people's pain and duplicitously pretend that he was the answer. The key to his success was the simple fact that he yelled angrily about this and bellowed out blame and false solutions like a carnival barker. He seemed angry, too, and people felt seen, even though he was acting in total self-interest, and shamelessly lied as he howled about wanting to help people. He deserves to be utterly condemned for this heinous pretense and the harm that he has continued to inflict on the very people that gravitated to him like confused moths to a radioactive, fake orange flame. However, this wouldn't have happened without the underlying, deep levels of angst and pain in the US.

The idea of simply going back to the way things were pre-Trump, doing the same things again and hoping for a different result, clearly will not get to the heart of the problem and fix it. The deep disillusionment and desperation in many parts of the country in 2016 is exactly what provoked the rise of this newly-emboldened, bitter, white, working class to rally behind the ugly, vitriolic messaging of the soon-to-be next President. Failure to address the issues of this time seems like a very poorly thought out remedy, doomed for failure, i.e. the re-election of Trump or an even more menacing demagogue in the near future.

I do remember saying way back in the early months of the Republican Primaries in 2015 when everyone started incessantly talking about Trump,

> *'Ignore him. He thrives on attention. Starve him of it and make him fade away into the irrelevance he deserves.'*

The DNC in 2016, led by Debbie Wasserman-Schultz, along with the Democratic campaign 'brains trust', Robbie Mook and John Podesta, didn't follow this approach as they made the concerted decision to elevate Trump as the 'pied piper' candidate, due to their avowed assertion that he couldn't win, so it would ensure an easy Democratic victory. Didn't quite work out as planned.

You've got to admit that Trump is a masterful showman with an uncanny knack for bringing out the most visceral reactions from many people, at both ends of the political spectrum. But this means he has almost everyone tuning in; deluded defenders and enraged opposers alike, and he, and the media world, are well aware of this. Hate viewing has become a new obsessive routine for a whole portion of the electorate who feel like they're doing their bit for democracy by tuning in for their daily fix of rage-watching to provide fodder for self-righteous water-cooler chats with vocally engaged political 'participants'.

> *'He's a loathsome offensive brute, and yet we can't look away!'*
> *(millennials might need to look up that reference).*

As best I can, I try to be a pragmatist. I see limited benefit in obsessing over problems, and rather prefer spending time working on solutions. I have never been able to become absorbed in watching or reading about the horrific shit-show that surrounds everything Trump does. He literally repulses me. I believe that way too many people focus too much on the multi-car pile-up at the notoriously dangerous Trump intersection; jumping around with their hair on fire, shrieking in consternation while transfixed on the damage, rather than arranging a group of concerned citizens to take a petition down to the local council office to get traffic lights put in, so as to avoid this daily recurrence of such unnecessary grief. This is my approach and is why I was in Iowa.

3.

IC minus 1: Lock in the Faithful, Persuade the Curious, and Avoid the Angsty

After a luxuriously deep sleep, with a shit-eating grin fixed on my noggin, I bounced out of my cheap and nasty hotel and set off on what was becoming a routine 6 or 7-hundred-metre morning stroll. This one was less terrifying. The sun was well up in small-town middle America and Cedar Rapids revealed itself to be a place of unlocked doors and super-friendly neighbours. Not convinced that I wanted another night in the same rat-trap, I again lugged my bags with me on my short trek. The snow outside was thigh deep between streets, but the footpath (sidewalk) would surely be clear.

Footpath?

This street wasn't made for walking, but that's just what I did - clambering across blizzard-stricken divisions between storage depot carparks, and sliding down arctic embankments into cheap housing driveways while Donkey Kong-ing my wheely bag over my head. All in the aforementioned snow that was comfortably above knee-height.

Confused onlookers seemed to be trying to decide if I was a casually dressed businessman who was lost, or a rather sharply dressed hobo just wandering around. It took a long time to get marginally closer to my goal before I embraced the best of my shitty options and decided to traipse along the side of this major road with vehicles hurtling past and spraying up gritty icy muck at me as I sloshed along in dirty curb slush. I was making progress, though. I was thankful that no-one stopped to offer me a ride, as I now must have looked like a recently busted unfaithful husband, who had scurried out of home at short notice under fire from an abuse-hurling wife and was now trying to hitch a ride to his brother Trevor's house in Minnesota to seek refuge before reassessing his damaged life.

Maybe they decided I didn't deserve a lift. They were probably right. I was in no position to argue. Trevor would understand. His wife, less likely.

Anyway, I knew I was getting close when I spied an approaching group of fresh-faced Bernie badge wearers, clipboards and flyers at the ready, embarking on their mission to lock in the faithful, persuade the curious, and avoid the angsty. After trading a few brief 'Go Bernies', I strode into Cedar Rapids' Bernie central command with a cheerful spirit, full heart, and only just socially acceptable amount of black ice melting into my jeans.

'Hi. What can I do to help?'

I was continually impressed with the instant recognition from pretty much all of the Bernie gang of my Aussie accent. Rarely even a guess, false speculation of Britishness, or unforgivable blunder into the scorn-worthy suggestion that I was a trans-Tasman rival. So, after a brief commendation for my un-likely journey - I spared them the details of my morning's icy escapades, but surely they had figured that out - I jumped at the chance to do some phone-banking until a vehicular escort could plonk me out in the action.

I think I go ok on the phones. I'm a good listener. Everyone just wants to be heard and understood. It's the inherent human quality that binds us all; self-importance. If you have the gall to bust into someone's life with an unprompted call, the least you can do is let them do most of the talking. Well-timed, appropriate questions; all of course working towards steering them in your desired direction – it's not just bloody therapy. Finding out what's important to people and then when the time is right, giving your own little insight into how your shared concerns have a common solution. Bernie has the solutions to almost every woe out there, which makes it an easy game.

The Aussie thing also came up a bit. I was still confused, be-cause in my life of living overseas, I regularly run into people who are impressively incapable of picking a Scotsman from a South African, let alone nailing which of the antipodean isles I was from in seconds.

Was it an Iowa thing? Can we thank Hugh Jackman? Al-though, when he said 'Crikey' for the 13th time in Baz Luhr-mann's 'Australia', I wanted a new accent. Anyway, you use what you can and this being-an Aussie-thing can occasionally be use-ful. The French, for example, don't hate us in the same way they reserve for the Brits and Yanks (Americans for those needing a little course on Australian lingo), if that's a good thing.

A couple of quick tips for our US cousins if you want to in-gratiate yourselves with those from Down Under - well firstly, don't say 'Down Under'. Also, hit the first syllable of 'Aussie' as though there is a famous wizard there. Not Harry Potter or Gandalf. Think Ozzie Osbourne and you'll be bang on. While we're at it, make the final syllable of Melbourne and Brisbane as short and unpronounced as humanly possible. Basically, shorten everything and abbreviate wherever you can, e.g.,

'In Straya, we like to kick a footy around in the arvo before grabbin' some Maccas and those choccie bikkies that were a Chrissie prezzie from Johnno'.

The fires in Australia at that time (early Feb, 2020) were uncontrollably savaging our nation and were commanding lead-story media attention globally. The footage of fire tornados and darkened daytime skies as people huddled on glowing beaches waiting to escape the approaching inferno by sea was truly frightening. Most conversations addressed this and made for a smooth transition into climate change discussions bringing about almost universally shared agreement that the world needs to pull its finger out of its arse (ass) and wake up to the startling reality that urgent change is needed. Bernie's Green New Deal proposal was the only policy, of the still many Dem candidates in the hunt, that offered an appropriately aggressive approach to giving human life on earth its best chance to continue to flourish. Fairly decent suggestion, avoiding inevitable catastrophe and potential extinction, if you really think about it, which clearly not enough people do.

Comparisons between Australia's universal public healthcare system and the US's insanely expensive, complicated, and inefficient set-up revealed that so many people were acutely (and chronically) sick of the American system and were in desperate need of a healthier one. People admitted that they knew the world was laughing at them for their backward, outdated, cruel healthcare system, or lack thereof. Again, Bernie was the only one standing on debate platforms, who truly supported a Medicare-for-all system to cover everyone in America at a cheaper overall cost. These people were low hanging fruit to become Bernie supporters. With the right information, almost everyone is. Sadly though, most of these people knew the problems, could ascribe basic steps about how to fix them, but mostly didn't know that Bernie was fighting for these exact measures that they were crying out for. Information is everything.

I enjoyed talking to people and tried to be as attentive, empathetic, and informative as I could. The only people still in the Bernie hut, not doing the rounds, were the campaign staff and most of them were silently working away on inputting and checking stuff online, leaving me as pretty much the lone voice in the room, other than some light chatter between the officials. This was a productive way to spend my first hour with the Bernie command team, as I went from a random Aussie bumbling in to being recognised as a knowledgeable and effective campaign operator. My hand was always up to assist in any way that I could.

I became a bit of a trusted go-to guy that was ready to tackle any odd job as required. Very happy to be in the thick of things.

Wendy was one of the first drop-off drivers to return after doing her own knock-around and bringing back her dropees. She'd moved up to Iowa a few years back from Texas to move in with a lad she'd met up with online. Things were going great and she deserved it. Sweet girl. She spoke just like a friend from Oz that I went through uni with, other than her soft Texan drawl. We had a brief, warm chat then she swung me out into the friendly, snowy streets of Cedar Rapids. I happily accepted her offer to stop off in a huge (yuppy-as-hell) wholefood market on the way, as she too was reluctant to live on donuts and Snickers bars throughout the duration of the campaign.

After nestling her delivery vehicle in the slushy carpark round the back, we sidled in through a rear door to enter right into the middle of a Tom Steyer rally with the eponymous candidate mid-speech about 15 metres from our entrance. Heads turned, maybe even Tom's. This was good, wholesome (bad pun intended) re-tail electioneering. Cheap seating had been set up and a couple of hundred punters were catching the Steyer show. More than half looked like they knew that this was happening, but a decent chunk of the rest looked like they just wanted a place to sit and launch into their quinoa and kale power-smoothies.

Tom Steyer is a very likeable, well-spoken fella, despite the fact that he became a billionaire on the back of heinous fossil fuel fracking businesses and diabolical private prisons. He now spoke out against these things, but I couldn't help but think his credibility on these issues was a tad compromised. He did sound genuine, though. However, there wasn't much chance of him snagging my support. A particular non-tainted non-billionaire spoke out against these horrendous issues more stridently and with an unimpeachable - would be nice if we could use that term in the presidential sense for the big, bad, Bernster - lifetime track record.

Still, I did bring back my organic 'Green Glow' mega-blend, filled with stuff like asparagus, spinach, broccoli, brussels sprouts, and alfalfa, and checked out the Steyerworks from pretty close up. I contentedly chewed into my pumpkin-seed encrusted hemp bun filled with beetroot, chia seeds, chickpeas, and lentils, or some such fart-fuelling mega-hipster concoction - named some-thing along the lines of 'Harmony Roll'. Despite the wankery, and corresponding prices, my body was craving to see a vegetable, as it had seen nothing but sugar-injected-fat-bombs for days, and

I didn't want it to forget how to digest vitamins and minerals. I felt energised as nutrition slid down my throat – like an ailing warrior in a fantasy computer game sculling a power potion that re-invigorated me back to maximum vitality. We hung around for a bit more Tom as we powered up - long enough for a gruff chap to bark orders at me,

> 'Get your ass out of my way,' after I'd paused for a few seconds at a good vantage point to get some snaps of the Steyermeister in action.

Unheard of in a Bernie crowd. Just sayin'. Anyway, he didn't strike me as an integral cog in the Steyer campaign, more like a meat-loving local farmer who was dragged into a 'healthy shit' shop by his nutrition-focused wife, and needed to lash out at someone 'cos he hadn't chewed into an animal for a couple of hours.

> 'Certainly, sir, and I hope you soon find a bloody piece of flesh to soothe your carnivorous withdrawal symptoms, for everyone's sake,' I didn't reply.

The people of Cedar Rapids made this chap look like an anomaly. It beats me how these people can keep such a welcoming disposition to the hordes of relentless campaign folks roaming the suburbs as if they were searching for a dangerous fugitive in hiding. It wasn't that uncommon to pass by a Warren-walker, Yang-banger, Pete-streeter, or Klob-trotter, following similar routes and leaving campaign paraphernalia on the same unanswered door handles.

Don't think I caught sight of the rare and elusive, at this stage looking deceptively endangered, Biden-backer, fired up and trying to remember an actual Biden policy, other than 'restoring the soul of the nation'. Plenty of evidence of Biden followers out there, although almost all were in the oldest demographic at this stage. It seemed these supporters mostly stayed indoors, out of range of potential contact with the concerns or perspective of anyone under 60. It was always entertaining to ask these Joe-faithful what their 3 favourite Biden policies were,

'Ok, how about 1?'

'Just the chance to listen to a President who isn't overtly rude.'

Pretty low bar. Similar questions could be posed to other candidate's supporters,

'Why Pete?'

'He's just so smart.'

'Sure, but how do his policies help you?'

'And really well dressed.'

Good, that's important.

There was some mild banter out there between rival campaign volunteers, and I saw plenty of other Bernie-bangers also engage in a bit of light-hearted heckling,

'Your flyers look heavy. Ours are much lighter. I've got plenty. Ditch those ones you've got and I'll give you a pile of mine,' and other feeble throwaway lines to fill the mildly awkward, literally icy-cold, air when passing by an enemy doorbanger.

These light-hearted jibes were enjoyed and returned by plenty of Yangers, a few Liz-lovers, the occasional Klob-nut, but not many of the Butt-heads (apologies, but hard to avoid), who seemed to take themselves way too seriously.

I enjoyed wandering around chatting to people, even though there were many unanswered knocks, unenthusiastic responses, as well as slippery paths, hard-to-get-to front doors, and gigantic over-friendly dogs (in almost every yard). Those who willingly engaged were thoughtful, responsive, eager to listen, and most of all kind-hearted. Lots of folksy well-wishes even from the non-Bernie locals. This was the kind of deluded and sweet answer that you could expect from this comfortably inert older crew,

'I'm an old guy that only watches cable news, so I'm unaware and have no concern for providing opportunities, like the ones I enjoyed, to anyone else to have a dignified life as was afforded me. I'll be doing as I'm told and will

be voting for Pete, Joe, or Amy, but I genuinely wish radical, old Bernie all the best for a loving and prosperous
future for him and all those dear to him.'

Good, healthy discussions with many. Everyone knew the
problems. Few had a firm grasp of potential solutions. Just getting that dangerous, rude, narcissist out of the White House was
a common refrain. I passionately agreed, except for the crucial
word 'just'.

At the end of the afternoon's door shift, Wendy swooped back
and scooped me up. She had to get home and it was in the other
direction from the Bernie base. Wendy had also volunteered to be
part of a caucus team and she had a quick prep meeting to go over
requirements. Would I mind joining her for her Caucus team's
pre-Caucus planning meeting? Sure.

The Caucuses are arcane, antiquated, complicated and, as
we were about to see close up tomorrow, have the potential to
be a colossal clusterfuck. It's no great surprise as there are 1,678
different sites plus 87 satellite caucuses scattered all over the
broad state, and each campaign should have a Precinct Captain
and support crew who knew what they were doing at every site,

ideally. She introduced me to her caucus mates and lamented the fact that her man was at work and wouldn't have a chance to meet an Aussie, which he would love as he is obsessed with all things Australian: animals, TV shows, music, etc. She showed me a gaudy, Aussie-themed mug of Jamie's, her fella, that read something along the lines of the deliberately misinterpretable,

'I love it Down Under.'

I was enjoying the Aussie-loving vibes, but was almost starting to wonder if I was in a Mid-Western version of The Truman Show where every actor was told to bang on about how much they liked Australia as the theme of this week's episodes. Anyway, it was nice.

One of the lads there was the only non-caucus virgin, but nor was he a caucus whore, so he was leading the way by piecing together what he remembered about the process and going through the official campaign literature about what to do. Quite complex; it felt a bit like a last-minute cram session for a test. I guess it kinda was, in a way. They seemed to get their plans pretty well under control, which was good; caucus day was tomorrow.

It was getting cold(er) and dark by the time I was deposited back into the Bernie hutch. After checking in and making sure all my voter contact details were entered into the system, I slunk across the road and grabbed a tasty Chinese feed at a restaurant at what I believe Americans call a 'strip mall', which never prove to be as exciting as they sound.

I dragged my stuff back along my icy commute to my familiar hotel, which somehow managed to get a few more stars in the ratings than it deserved. Settling into my room, where the much-needed heater was being intermittently agreeable, I tried to convince myself that watching the Superbowl would captivate my attention. It didn't.

Still clothed and hugging as many bedsheets and blankets as I could to avoid frostbite, I caught up with some correspondence before drifting off to a chilly, but reasonably restful, sleep.

C. Mini-rant 3 – Simply Going Back to 2016 would be like Giving Tylenol for a Virus

The failure of the Dems in 2016 has been attributed to many things, but one inescapable reality is that Trump's bid, despite all its ugliness, was definitely the 'change' campaign. His victory, against so many rational reasons for him to fail, again revealed the deep levels of dissatisfaction felt by the US electorate. It was also a sad repudiation of the much heralded 'hope and change' of 2008. If the Dems had backed up their rhetoric and truly had the back of the working class, they would have been unbeatable. If.

It is time for the Democratic Party to stand up for middle and working class needs with a substantive jobs program to rebuild the nation's crumbling infrastructure and to aggressively transition to renewable energy, as well as invest in building affordable housing. Combine this with:

- *increasing the national minimum wage from the paltry $7.25 per hour to at least 15 bucks an hour (tied to inflation)*
- *strengthening trade unions to fight for worker benefits and protections*
- *reforming the racist criminal justice system and abolishing private, for-profit prisons*
- *installing a universally-guaranteed public healthcare system*
- *and low-cost public childcare*

as well as:

- *humane immigration reform*
- *strengthened women's and LGBTQ+ rights*
- *proper maternity and paternity leave*
- *robust rent controls*
- *sturdy reinvestment into education*
- *free public universities and the cancellation of student debt*
- *national legalisation of marijuana*
- *significantly reducing foreign military interventionism*
- *and so on*

All of these things are absolutely achievable in the richest country in the history of the world.

Changes to the individual and corporate tax codes are required that would only affect the tiniest number of those right at the very tippy top of the economic ladder, who have been making out like bandits and already have billions of excess wealth that could not be spent by generations of the most extravagant attempts by future family. This uber-excessive wealth has been taken out of the economy and stashed in off-shore accounts. Close those loopholes, make the exorbitantly-wealthy pay tax on this. The highest levels of the marginal tax rate don't even need to be increased much, and only for those making more than 5, 10, 20 million bucks a year, or more. Put in a minuscule tax on every Wall St. transaction and rein in bloated military budgets while you're at it and there is easily enough money to fundamentally strengthen the system for ALL.

A mere return to how things were in 2016 or before without addressing the fundamental rot in the system would be like giving a painkiller to someone with a malignant disease and telling them that everything will be ok. It would mask the pain, but the damage would still eat away at the fabric of a civilised society continuing to break down.

A simple rewind to the conditions of pre-Trump America would be an ineffective painkiller; like prescribing Tylenol to treat a disease.

4.

Iowa Caucus Day: We Must Get Someone to Fix These

I woke early as the heater, installed sometime in the 70s and never attended to since, sputtered either on or off, not to regulate the temperature, but rather because its internal wiring had gone insane. It was cold and the heater's schizophrenic attempts weren't helping, so I decided to rug up (more) and wander down to take advantage of one of the world's worst free breakfasts. Shitty thermos coffee, stale white bread for toasting and those shallow little sachets filled with strawberry jam that is always reluctant to leave its cosy corners. Along with cereal that had been in cylindrical dispensing tubes since at least the previous Iowa caucuses and was no doubt chosen by an 8-year-old kid - multi-coloured artificiality in many different shapes and sizes. I settled for just the camping-style coffee and fibreless toast with congealed red food colouring on top. Good to start the day like a king!

There was a chap, about my age, who'd also been there the previous morning, and who chatted in an almost flirty way with the usual girl on the front desk, which adjoined the small, poorly maintained breakfast zone. He perhaps lived there, such was his lame over-familiarity, which didn't seem to bother her in the slightest. Her retorts were hardly gonna land her a plush gig on a high-rating variety show, or the after-dinner talk circuit.

The lad, who was the only other soul brave enough to take on the assorted disappointments arrayed in the self-serve mini-cafeteria, seemed intent on making the most of it with numerous well-stocked cups, plates, and bowls piled up on the table in front of him. I quickly learned that this was a strategic decision. He'd doubled up on everything, knowing full well that his ingestion success rate was at about 50% - alternating randomly between failed and completed consumption attempts.

He seemed to possess few discernible signs of any acquired mealtime motor skills. Every attempted sip of coffee left roughly equal amounts agreeably transferred into his mouth, as were spilled onto shirt, table, jeans, and/or floor in a way that seemed so predictable that he barely bothered to notice or care. It was only when he deposited bits of shiny cereal on himself, sticking to his clothes like the cheapest sequined Mardi Gras costume imaginable, that prompted him to comment, probably only because I was there doing my best not to gape at every woeful effort to achieve an effective mouthful,

'Ah, it's just one of those mornings.'

Yesterday morning was also one of those mornings, and I was beginning to suspect that every morning might be.

The poor fella didn't seem to be drunk. That was the most logical conclusion and I had been investigating that possibility since I first encountered him the previous morn. I'd engaged him in a reasonable amount of frivolous banter and his speech wasn't affected - no shameless slurring, certainly not to the extent that should accompany the level of drunkenness required to match such minimal levels of co-ordination. He spoke cogently, was well-balanced, and there was no smell of alcohol; he just seriously struggled to get food into his gob. In fact, he was a world leader in the art, usually lost in the mid-to-late toddler years, of shovelling food all over himself.

At first, I avoided commenting on his YouTube-viral-hit level of personal mess-making, which had me enthralled despite my weak attempts not to stare. I had to restrain my urge to applaud some of his more spectacular failed attempts. After a bit, though, I felt the need to offer some unconvincing words of encouragement when he would drop a spoon into his paper coffee cup, knocking it over his toast which he'd pick up and the soggy remains would then slip through his fingers into his cereal, splashing kaleido-scopic milk up all over the table and his lap,

'Oooh, unlucky,' which brought earnest nods in response as if he agreed that yet again fate had conspired against him.

The young lass at the front desk, whom I presume played a major role in cleaning up this one-man food fight, seemed unper-turbed by the whole slapstick display of breakfast destruction - a performance that would have made The Three Stooges proud. I continued to offer the occasional half-hearted,

'That one was close. Nearly got it,' as if success was, per-haps, just one more errant spoonful away.

It wasn't.

I bade him a cheery farewell and authentic wishes of good luck; seemed like he'd had a pretty rough go of things. I was a little curious about his past, but didn't feel right inquiring too deeply into his stories of yesteryear over weak coffee and stale toast. Nor did I want to further distract his concentration from his task at hand - valiantly trying to get enough fuel into his body for his day ahead.

My door card was playing up, again, so I informed the girl in charge and she seemed to grab a random collection of identical looking cards from other room slots. From the half-deck of cards, none of them worked. This prompted a mini-spiel of feigned surprise and mutterings about faulty magnetic strips. I presumed she'd been giving the same little blurb to other guests outside their rooms, for weeks, months or maybe longer, such was the lack of heart or conviction in her well-practised bewilderment. She shuffled the cards and tried again and after much jiggling one of them finally did the trick,

>'There you go. We must get someone to fix these,' she said, looking at me with an expression that revealed that we both knew that wasn't going to happen.

I embarked on my now routine jaunt down to the field office and was beginning to find my ice legs. It was a bit earlier than the day before as I wanted to make sure that I hitched a ride out in the first wave. I realised that this wasn't going to be a problem as my target came into view - the place was bristling with life. People were milling about outside as there didn't seem to be enough room to fit everyone indoors. It was caucus day, after all, and people were buzzing as I started engaging,

>'Wow! Great turnout today.'

>'Yeah, was incredible to see Bernie up close. I shook his hand, and Sarah got a selfie.'

>'Hey?'

>'You just missed him. He and Jane popped through to give us a caucus day fire up.'

>'Brilliant. Must've been amazing. Bugger.'

Despite living in East Asia for close to 2 decades, the global heartland of selfies (Koreans had a word for it well before the West – 'selca,' an abbreviation of 'self-camera'), I never got swept up by the local enthusiasm, so getting a snap with Bernie wasn't high on my agenda for this trip. Yet this near miss, along with my budding selfie collection started just a few days before, got me thinking. It would be pretty cool to shake his hand and maybe even sneak in a little shot together with him. It wouldn't be easy, though, as most there missed out - in a manner similar to the chap's stomach at my recent breakfast. Anyway, the idea lurked in the back of my mind and I remembered some pre-trip discussions with mates who had floated the idea of getting some mini mementos to mark my trip. Would be great if I get the chance. We'll see how it goes.

The word of the main attraction's morning appearance was sent through about an hour before his arrival and everyone was asked to stay around - surely without much need to press the point.

Most had already arranged their runs, so I did the same and teed up a lift with another young couple, Taylor and Hayley, and was dropped back out in the streets for a final hit-out in Iowa.

The doors were a dream today, as we were in full mobilisation mode, meaning that only designated Bernie supporters were on our lists. The daily mission was to make sure they were ready to go: knew where to be, when, and had transport lined up. The previous lists were a combination of mostly Democrat or Dem-leaning voters and then a pile of unknowns, so it was about information gathering. We were also encouraged to have persuasive chats, putting forward Bernie's case to the undecided for at least a few minutes. Today was different. It was about speed and hitting up as many of the Bernie faithful as possible, to keep them on track and ensure a high turnout.

Very rewarding work. Lots of high-fiving, mutual cheers and hollered encouragement. Abounding positive energy was behind every door. I could've kept knocking on those doors forever, as the emotional lift of so many inspiring people was a joy to be a part of.

As the afternoon lengthened, I got myself back into the central shed and followed up on my morning enquiry to find a lift across more lengthy plains to Des Moines, where Bernie's results watch party would be. I was given the tip that John from Boston might be my huckleberry, so I gave him a call.

Full car.

Bummer.

After another quick room announcement brought no joy, I contemplated hitching until one girl showed such concern that I decided against putting her through any more angst. Minutes later, a fresh road gang returned from their street crusade. It was the Philly DSA (Democratic Socialists of America) crew: Jeremy, Ann, Trevor, and Josh. They were already squeezed into their petite hire car. Could they also wedge in an Aussie wayfarer looking to hitch onto their tiny wagon?

'Hang on. Might need to rearrange some bags.'

Their weekender luggage barely fit into the rear storage area without my international contributions, and it looked grim. But with gung-ho commitment to helping out another true believer, Jeremy, the talisman of the team, Tetris-ed all the bags into the minuscule hatch-back, including mine.

We were all set. After wrapping up a quick final flurry of late-afternoon caucus day doors, we set forth for Des Moines, incapable of seeing anything out of the back of the clown car.

At the risk of getting repetitive, these guys were gems; sharp, funny, hyper-informed, and great company. They were frontline troops for progressive change. DSA had surged since Bernie's last run and were forming deep, long-term networks. It wasn't the last of my encounters with DSA soldiers. Engrossing and enlightening discussions shrunk the vast plains of Iowa and we got there early to join the growing queue to share enthusiastic banter about Bernie's chances. Looked like Bernie was on deck, too, as the 'Not me, Bus' was already here at the Des Moines Airport Convention Center and Hotel for Bernie's official campaign results watch party.

At this stage I had only a few of what was to become an extensive collection of Bernie buttons - the badges that volunteers wear and freely hand out. They are spat out of manual presses in assembly-line quantities in campaign hot zones and people are encouraged to take a pile and share them widely. I was keeping one of each different design and my numbers were just warming up, ranging from standard-issue to mega-hippy.

I emptied my buttons and some pens from my jacket pocket and passed through the metal detector beepless. It would be an hour or two before any real results would start coming through and hours more before proceedings would officially begin. All the media giants were getting set up, and there were lots of recognisable faces, as everyone else was making plentiful trips to the conveniently located inside bar.

I'd just like to point out here that major media - TV, radio, and print - should not escape some accountability for Trump's success. Across the board they shamefully basked in the inflated ratings (a boon for these endangered industries) from those both devoted to and repulsed by the imbecilic buffoon. They hyper-focused on, and thus elevated, the grotesque Trump circus with all its inherent dangers, in the name of boosting their ratings (and enhancing some mutual big business interests).

The CEO of CBS, Leslie Moonves, gave us a little peek behind the curtain in early 2016 when he said the quiet part out loud, with perhaps regrettable honesty,

'It may not be good for America, but it's damn good for CBS.'

At the 2018 White House Correspondents' Dinner, comedian Michelle Wolf, while excoriating the absent maggot-in-chief, also took a valid swing at the assembled, highly-paid media talking heads, by pointing out,

'You guys are obsessed with Trump. Did you used to date him? Because you pretend like you hate him, but I think you love him. I think what no one in this room wants to admit is that Trump has helped all of you. He couldn't sell steaks or vodka or water or college or ties or Eric, but he has helped you. He's helped you sell your papers and your books and your TV. You helped create this monster, and now you're profiting off of him. If you're going to profit off of Trump, you should at least give him some money, because he doesn't have any.'

In her humorous, but harsh, critique of the insanity of the current administration, she also took a little swipe at Sarah Huckabee Sanders, who was deputised to stand in for the sulking little Donnie boy. The very same media who devote their entire existence these days to full-frontal attacks on Trump and all his acolytes, somehow deemed this to be crossing the line. They completely misrepresented what Wolf said, suggesting that she'd made a gross personal attack on SHS's appearance. This is what she said,

> 'I actually really like Sarah. I think she's very resourceful. She burns facts, and then she uses that ash to create a perfect smoky eye. Like maybe she's born with it, maybe it's lies. It's probably lies.'

This was lambasted across media left and right as an unacceptable attack. I don't remember seeing a line to avoid crossing before or after when it came to dishing out daily public lashings to Trump and his lackeys, which was ratings gold. It was open season for this. Was the line she actually crossed the one where you expose the hypocrisy of big media directly to their face? She also wrapped up her comedic blurb by doing a better job than the recalcitrant big media and government alike by bringing attention to the should-be front-page-national-shame-daily fact that,

> 'Flint still doesn't have clean water.'

This made the applause from the faux-chastened crowd of overpaid corporate mouthpieces even more muffled as she brought further focus on the fact that they are incapable of sufficiently addressing the right things.

Larry Wilmore, as the guest speaker at the same press dinner a few years before, suffered a similar backlash when he also made rather pointed remarks about the inadequacies of the media, and threw in a predator drone reference about Obama, to boot.

'Saw you hangin' out with NBA players like Steph Curry; Golden State Warriors. That was cool, that was cool, yeah. You know it kinda makes sense, too, because both of you like raining down bombs on people from long distances, right, yeah, sir? What, am I wrong? What?

Speaking of drones, how is Wolf Blitzer still on television? Ask a follow-up question? Good lord. Hey, Wolf, I'm ready to project tonight's winner; anyone who isn't watching the Situation Room.'

A frosty reception. You'd think someone called Wolf would have developed a sense of self-deprecating humour over a lifetime of over-exposure. Apparently not.

Wilmore was fired from Comedy Central a few months later - they cancelled 'The Nightly Show' which he hosted. Maybe both he and Wolf (the one with the shrieky, non-monotone voice, that is) were a little too close to the bone. Some things are just off limits.

The growing numbers at the Bernie results party were mingling around chatting as if we were at a staff Christmas party where everyone got on famously - straight into mutually understood gossip, analysis, and speculation (introductions were an occasional afterthought). Independent media were all around, too, and this lot were far more willing to mill about in the crowd, both chatting and sometimes getting recorded interviews going. I happened past Emma Vigeland, the ever-excellent video journalist for The Young Turks, and blurted out,

'Emma Vigeland, you rock!'
She hit me back with a warm,

'Thanks, buddy,' and gave me a quick, firm handshake to confirm the moment, yet again showing that everything she does, she does well.

After a quick, relieving trip to the facilities, I turned back towards the main hall when I heard the distinctive laughter of another favourite journalist of mine, and jerked my head around to confirm that it was, indeed, Matt Taibbi. I'd been reading his insightful and amusing articles in Rolling Stone magazine for years and had seen him interviewed a number of times. His laugh was easy for me to pick because I've checked out plenty of episodes of himself and Katie Halper doing their weekly gig 'Useful Idiots' - either on YouTube or their corresponding podcast. He was taken aback when I swung my head around to gawk at him from just a few metres away, so I averted my gaze and continued on my way. I would get another chance to have a brief chat with him later on what turned out to be a long day.

Jordan Chariton was conducting some interviews near the entrance to the main hall, and I couldn't help but walk behind one of his interviewees and sneak a furtive glance up at the camera on my way past. One of my mates is a big fan and I let him know that I might be spottable in the backdrop of an upcoming interview, which proved to be true.

Without any doubt, though, the highlight of this mingling was when Nina Turner came out to share some love with the crew on the floor. I waited until the right time and then engaged her with some heartfelt thanks and praise,

'You, too, baby.'

'After Bernie's last go-around, Nina, I started up an Our Revolution group in South Korea where I live to keep our gang together and carry on the progressive momentum we'd built up.'

'Good for you, man.'

'I was watching you being interviewed by Cenk on TYT a few years back and you were talking about the hundreds and hundreds of Our Revolution groups springing up all over the US. You then said, "There are also some international groups popping up in places like France and even one in South Korea". I yelped with joy when I heard this and my wife ran into the room to make sure I was ok. I told her, "Nina just mentioned our local Our Revolution group". I was pretty happy.'

'That is great to hear. Keep up your excellent work. I'm proud of you.'

'Thanks, that means a lot to me'.

And it did.

Those assembled represented a committed group of progressives. Activist groups who were siloed into their own specific causes when Bernie had a crack at the big job in 2016, have since come together to form progressive coalitions.

It had become apparent that these groups shared fundamental goals, striving to further gender, racial, LGBTQ+, social, economic, and environmental interests. These had been increasingly marginalised by an uncaring profit-seeking system. So, as well as Bernie shirts and buttons (badges), there were many similar items showing mutual support for Black Lives Matter, National Nurses United, Code Pink, American Postal Workers Union, ACLU, the Sunrise Movement, and so on. Through my ongoing schmoozing, I discovered that many present were integral members of these groups and their organisational structure. The overwhelming number of those I engaged with reflected an impressive level of knowledge and capability. These would be ideal folks to speak to the media about why they were here and what moral-based goals they were hoping that the Sanders candidacy would help them to achieve.

In a crowd of perhaps a couple of thousand, there were obviously going to be a few in the midst who were not quite as capable of showing such calm, rational, highly-informed approaches as required to be media savvy. At the risk of sounding like Larry David in a scene from Curb Your Enthusiasm, I noticed that when big media operators made rare forays into the fray with cameras in tow, they liked to choose someone from this tiny pool of less conventional supporters. It seemed as if they were cherrypicking the nutters to talk to. I mentioned this to the fellow I was chatting with, and he replied with a straight-faced lack of surprise by stating,

> 'Same thing last time. Always seem to pick out the odd-balls to represent the campaign. You think perhaps they might be trying to put forward a negative narrative?', he said rhetorically.

Print media were a little less discerning when they wandered around looking for quotes, but, with a few exceptions, most of the questions I heard, and occasionally received, struck me as a little loaded,

> 'Will you vote for an establishment candidate if Sanders doesn't win the nomination?', was the opening question I received from Howard Fineman (writer for Real Clear Politics) at a rally in New Hampshire the following week, just after he established that I was Australian.

> 'Gonna be tricky to vote for anyone, as an Australian.'

> 'Oh, yeah, right. Do you think these other Bernie folks will?'

> 'You might be better off asking them. Plenty around. Do you wanna know why I travelled across the world to volunteer for Bernie?'

'Ah, ok, sure,' he said, unconvincingly, but I'd cornered him a little and I presume he didn't want to give his honest response, which I can only speculate to have been,

'Actually, I just want a couple of direct quotes to aid the framing of my piece which I've already determined to be focused on Sanders supporters being recklessly dedicated to destroying the Democratic Party.'

I disappointed him by giving my well-worked spiel, pretty smoothly and effectively, I thought. He looked rather distracted throughout as he seemed to be looking around for people who might jump into his poorly-hidden trap. The far more common and prescient talking points that almost every Sanders supporter readily, often unprompted, provided was their empathetic concern about how to engender greater opportunities for all - explained with detailed understanding of the issues and policies to remedy them, combined with personal anecdotes to capture why they are so important to them, brimming with the heart, passion, and love that had stirred them out of their comfort zone to devote time and energy to the Sanders campaign.

'Not interested,' was the feeling I got back when these responses were heard by those with corporate agendas to push.

He pretended to jot down some notes and then shuffled off looking for an elusive target foolish enough to jump in front of his loaded question, incongruously asked at the time when Bernie was the frontrunner, no less.

One such media target at the Bernie Iowa results party, was a lady whose passion was teetering a bit too close to the edge of sanity. She was wearing this button (pictured) that I thought worthy of commenting on to her, at which point she brought one out of her pocket at gunslinger speed and handed it to me. I quite liked it, but stashed it away from prying media and would only bring it out for trusted eyes (like yours now). I wandered off to more productive conversations, but I did notice her getting her moment in the spotlight a little later as she was giving an intense, slightly unhinged, interview to a gleeful camera crew.

As results started rolling in, live feeds from the room were beamed through CNN and were simultaneously shown up on the big screens in the venue. I was standing next to Trevor, the tallest person in the room, who was also wearing the loudest hat - a luminescent, orange beanie. Thus, it was very easy to pick us out in the crowd. A politically like-minded girl I work with, Jess, who didn't know I was there, sent me an excited message,

'You've snuck yourself into a Bernie event in Iowa, haven't you? Just saw you on CNN.'

I replied with this photo:

I was text chatting with a few others, including my mum (mom), and after pointing out that I was adjacent to the loftiest lad in attendance, who was sporting bright orange, pop-pom-topped headwear, I received a surge of confirmed sightings.

It was close. Very close. Bernie and Pete were level pegging and as the evening panned out, it became obvious that the overall state delegate count to go to the convention would be equal overnight even though Bernie had over 6,000 more first round votes - a lead he never relinquished.

A tie then, unless you need to anoint a winner, which the media's horse-race-reporting style salivates for. As has happened when delegate counts have been shared in previous contests, the person with more votes is deemed to be the winner. This was the determinative metric focused on just 4 years ago when the final voting percentage revealed a close Hillary victory 49.84% to Bernie's 49.59%. However, before it got too late and viewers went to bed and while the reality of the evening was that it was at least too close to call, Mayor Pete jumped onto his lectern and announced in a live broadcast to all networks that he had won. Well, he's young and maybe brash, so the media would surely rap him over the knuckles for falsely claiming this win. Right?

Well, suddenly there was great talk of SDEs as the agreed upon way to determine the winner. You know SDEs, yeah? State Delegate Equivalencies, the infinitely complicated precinct level breakdown of delegate quotas before they get ushered into larger delegate pools. It's not just that people didn't understand them, very few people were aware that they even existed. Also, vote tallying had broken down, just as Buttigieg had snuck into a minuscule SDE lead. That is, the tallying using the untested and prophetically-named Shadow Inc. app that was introduced a couple of days before the caucuses by the DNC as per recommendations from the Buttigieg team, which had concerning overlapping connections,

> 'Shadow Inc. developed software for the campaigns of numerous Democratic candidates.[3][35] The Joe Biden, Pete Buttigieg and Kirsten Gillibrand presidential campaigns all made payments to the company.[3][5] The Buttigieg campaign paid $42,500 to the company in July 2019 for "software rights and subscriptions" for a text-message service.[3] The Biden campaign paid the company $1,225, also for a text-messaging service,[36] while the Gillibrand campaign paid $37,400 the company for software and fundraising consulting.[37]' (Wikipedia)

The tally stopped at a point where the Pete campaign had just inched ahead in this hyper-bureaucratic metric. And 'Buttigieg narrowly wins Iowa' was the prevalent headline and lead story in the morning. A bit fishy to say the least. About 3 or 4 days later when counting resumed and got up into 90+ percent, Sanders had wrested back the lead in this esoteric SDE category, as well as still comfortably leading the overall vote count. But by then the dominant Iowa narrative was that it was a complete balls-up and that Buttigieg was the winner. Momentum blunting stuff.

It was the satellite caucuses that were the last to be tallied and these were often in the remotest parts of the state, usually at a workstation, like an abattoir where migrant workers were located and couldn't get to any other caucus site. Bernie smashed home victories in these satellites and they were set to push him into a stable win in the SDEs, as well. But the DNC cancelled any more vote tallying and said it was too late and too complicated by then. This rendered these most marginalised of groups to be disenfranchised. Just about sums up the migrant experience in the US - not being factored into top level interests, ignored by the media, and a total disregard shown for their democratic rights.

The Iowa caucuses were aptly described as being an utter shitshow and perhaps even a tangled morass, a little ironic considering the relevant entry in Wikipedia regarding the Shadow Inc. technology,

> 'The Iowa Democratic Party paid Shadow Inc. $63,183 to develop the IowaReporterApp.[18] Before the 2020 Iowa caucus, the app and its developer were kept secret from the public by the Democratic party, although it was made public that there would be an app used for the caucus.[19] [8] The company published a new build (Version 1.1) of the IowaReporterApp two days before the caucuses.[20] A bug in the code of the app[21] caused the app to fail at the time of the 2020 Iowa Democratic caucuses.[22] Gerardo Niemira, the CEO of Shadow Inc., which created the

app, stated that technology used by Democrats in prior elections was a "shitshow" and "tangled morass".[23]'

The DNC at its finest ineptitude - top-shelf incompetence at best, and skullduggery at worst. Hard to unravel all the levels of failure and get your head around how, with 4 years to prepare, it was all rushed in at the last minute without anyone having a practical understanding of how it worked. Wikipedia continues,

'Not-for-profit ProPublica commissioned a security audit of the app. It was determined to be "insecure," so an external entity could have hacked it.[27][28]

The app was reviewed by the Democratic National Committee in advance. David Bergstein said on behalf of the DNC that it was confident that security was being taken "extremely seriously."[29]

Several security and app experts have criticized the amateurish nature of the app.[30] App-development expert, Kasra Rahjerdi, said "the app was clearly done by someone following a tutorial. It's similar to projects I do with my mentees who are learning how to code." A team of researchers at Stanford University, including former Facebook chief security officer Alex Stamos, said that while analyzing the app, they found potentially concerning code within it, including hard-coded API keys.[31]'

The head of the Iowa DNC was hung out to dry as the designated fall guy (falling on his sword for recompense down the track, I'd suggest) and the show moved on.

After another official recount, it was declared that Buttigieg had indeed won by 2 state delegates over Bernie, but formal complaints of unrecorded satellite caucuses and multiple discrepancies across the board were lodged (consistently at Sanders' expense, as it turns out). To this day, they are still pending and have been left unresolved. Time for all to cut their losses and move on, except Buttigieg who amidst all the confusion and shitfuckery (shout-out to Honest Government Ads from the brilliant Aussie 'The Juice Media'), preened about like the winner from well before he had any right to do so.

At the results watch party, Bernie came out and spoke with characteristic humility and composure, just after Mayor Pete had completely inappropriately stolen the limelight. In a way that the rest of us cannot possibly try to imagine, Bernie has been pushing against these institutional advantages that have been stacked against him for decades and was far better equipped to keep his cool when, yet again, powerful forces seemed to align against him.

Having said that, he did look and sound a little pissed off. This was, of course, not the Bernie speech that I had come there to see.

As confusion reigned and the evening dragged on, a smorgasbord of Sanders surrogates graced the stage with tales of courage and commitment about unwavering resilience and resolve. Nina had taken up the role of MC and was wheeling out a full array of the team to keep the show rolling as everyone waited to see if any more tallies would come in and a more definitive result for the evening could be determined.

Beers flowed, and discussions increased in liveliness. To be fair, all the Bernie fans I knew had developed thick skins from last time around and the key was not to let frustrations boil over into either angst-ridden online venting (seized upon as examples of 'Bernie Bro' behaviour, even when coming from a 58-year-old African American woman) or despair.

Trying to beat the DNC-ordained candidates was like playing the All Blacks at Eden Park with Richie McCaw in control of the whistle (trying to beat a Tom Brady team when he's also refereeing the game).

Tough. You just had to keep turning up and doing your best.

It was a good crew to be with now as things remained remarkably upbeat; reminiscent of a sporting crowd gathered to watch the first game of a long series which was tied in overtime pending an inquiry. Regardless of this result, there was a long road ahead and optimism was high because we were a well-trained team of fresh-faced players who would only get stronger with time. This vibe was eventually, and very slowly, ushered outside to the front of the building, once it was comfortably past midnight and it became clear that no further results would be forthcoming tonight.

D. Mini-rant 4 – Bernie Knows the Cure

The fundamental problems in the system need to be rebalanced away from extreme corporate control back to supporting opportunities for people. This would not require radical changes, just a return to the policies that were wildly successful and overwhelmingly popular from not long after the 1929 depression through until the 1970s, when the much-heralded American Dream was a reality.

This was the period when people had well-paid, stable jobs, affordable housing, and solid public infrastructure to support them (well, white people, at least). The many Northern European countries which retain these platforms today, routinely dominate the global list as the happiest nations on earth. Reverting to the tax codes of this era (no need to go anywhere near as far as having the highest tax rate at 91%, as it was under the Republican Presidency of Dwight Eisenhower), along with scaling back obscenely bloated and wasteful military spending, and implementing a very small Wall St. transaction tax will provide ample funds to be reinjected into the economy (and this is without even bringing MMT – Modern Monetary Theory - into the discussion. Look up Stephanie Kelton for more info on this). These vast resources can then be used to strengthen basic public programs like education, healthcare, infrastructure, and renewable energy programs (creating countless jobs).

This is all Bernie proposes. He is an FDR-style New Deal Democrat. He bravely, perhaps foolishly, describes his politics as Democratic Socialism, which sadly brings about confused, often media-heightened, pejorative suggestions of pure socialism – meaning the state fully takes over and controls the means of production – which he is not suggesting at all. This also gets conflated with ludicrous assertions that he supports communism with fanciful comparisons to authoritarian dictatorships like Stalin in the USSR; perversely seen as not being out of bounds in the distorted, sensationalised US media landscape.

Sanders promotes the same policies that were very successfully employed by most of the Western World during the sizeable middle chunk of last century, when things were 'great'. I recently heard Chomsky describe these exact, Keynesian economic policies as 'morally-regulated capitalism', which is the way I prefer to describe them. They result in much more disposable income ending up in working and middle-class hands, which then gets put back into the economy; creating more jobs, entrepreneurial opportunities, and strengthening small and medium-sized businesses (rather than having vast wealth at the top taken out of the economy and getting stashed into havens, trust funds, stocks etc). This middle-out economics (not the thoroughly debunked trickle-down concept) is better for everyone in the 99.99%, that is all but the owners of gigantic business empires, often multi-national conglomerates, who are already swimming in such excessive wealth that they are incapable of spending it. Thus, Bernie is the cure.

The progressive platform put forward by Senator Sanders is the vaccine for a disease-ridden system in desperate need.

PART 2

Countdown to the New Hampshire Primary

1.

NHP minus 6: Conviviality, Camaraderie, and Rapport

Beers started to kick in for many as there was singing, dancing, and general cavorting in front of the Des Moines Airport Convention Center and Hotel. We chanted an uplifting round of 'Bernie, Bernie...' at the 'Not Me, Bus' as it took him and Jane away to re-energise and rally for the ongoing fight. I had no accommodation lined up and no fixed plans, so eagerly joined the Philly DSA and friends as they trooped off to The Thirsty Sportsman bar to meet up with a pile of comrades from the corresponding New York DSA chapter to carry revelry deeper into the night.

Awesome fun. I was making heaps of new friends and contact details were being liberally shared and not left dormant as it is always a pleasure to share the occasional comment with those who you know to be on the exact same political wavelength.

Fun people, raucous tales, campaigning anecdotes - lively merriment all round.

The manager of The Thirsty Sportsman was a large, knock-about guy who wouldn't have looked out of place if you'd perched him up in the bleachers at a Nascar Rally with one of those beer hats with 2 straws curling down into his piehole for an idle afternoon consuming repetitive sport and warm, flat, tasteless lager. I was conscious not to spout too much shameless pinko rhetoric within earshot of his gracious, steady distribution of purchased ales to the assembled brigade. So I was gratified when I heard him chime in to another conversation with a perceptive observation that would have made Karl Marx proud. I thought we were there 'cos it was the only bar open at 2am, but maybe there was more to it. I opened up and engaged the burly barman and he was full of pearls of progressive wisdom, spoken with the throaty brogue of a man who sounded like he was used to barking orders during long stints at sea. He was a solid lad in every sense of the word. I imagine it wasn't every night that he got to immerse himself in deep discourse on the frailties of the capitalist model and how it could be effectively reformed.

It was a cavernous bar resplendent with a half dozen pool tables, dart boards, basketball shooting games, and an area dedicated to cornholing. Or playing with your cornhole. Or cornhole tossing. I wasn't quite sure of the correct terminology, but it was a game that I would find myself playing soon enough in an indoor sports arena in New Hampshire.

But I'm getting ahead of myself. The Thirsty Sportsman also had screens ranging from sizeable to gigantic, seemingly showing every live sporting fixture that was taking place anywhere on the globe. I hope I'm wrong, but I'm guessing the regular clientele that piles in to this recreational wet dream after a hard day's yakka (work) rarely launches into symposiums on the teachings of Trotsky. Right now, however, it was a perfect storm of beer, sport, and politics.

It ticked over to become my birthday, as it had been in Korea and Australia since before lunch on the previous day here (when my wife called me). I kept this to myself, as it seemed an unnecessary indulgence that would've felt like a distraction from a day of shared ideals. Nonetheless, I started receiving a few more messages and calls as Australia and Korea were waking up. It was one of the more festive birthday celebrations I'd had in a while, even though all of the 'guests' present were totally unaware. I couldn't imagine many other scenarios where I would be on the other side of the world to all my loved ones, both family and friends, on my birthday and yet was rejoicing the day with sincere conviviality, camaraderie, and rapport. It was a bit strange, and I did miss my wife, but I was truly happy.

We then moseyed off to a 24-hour family restaurant, an Arby's or Applebee's or IHOP (which took me years to learn was an acronym and not quite as ridiculous a name as I'd thought; like Apple's new computerised pogo stick, perhaps). We piled in and set up camp in the middle of about 15 more of the DSA inner circle, who were already gorging themselves on bland diner-style meals with accompanying animated and snappy exchanges. They all seemed to know each other well enough to unfurl friendly ribbing and gibes that were received with buoyant, cognisant approval all around. They seemed like a tight bunch. I'd been told that the NY and Philly chapters of DSA had teamed up to work together in moving toward their mutual political mission, but was now realising that they'd hung out a lot socially, too. I liked them.

I ended up sitting next to an fun and lively lass, who I later found out was a former Hollywood B-movie vixen. After an unconventional career transition, she'd become a leftie journo with an entertaining and popular Twitter presence. I'm a reluctant tweeter, but do check in daily to see what my extensive range of followed political commentators and news organisations find to be tweetable. She asked me for my Twitter handle (a question which I would sound self-conscious trying to pull off). I told her mine then asked,

'What's yours?'

'Lefty-Desiree McLeftyFace Slaps back w/ Milkshakes.'

'No shit? I've seen your mischievous work in action plenty of times - ripping in and taking down all who deserve it,' I spouted.

Her Twitter name was instantly recognisable; impossible to remember, but easy to spot. She explained the name, which she'd amended to send it up a right wing nutjob who was hounding her online. Her 'handle' gives an accurate indication of the type of person she is - funny, dynamic, and boisterous company.

The 3 or 4 crowded tables of Berners were heaving with energy. Absolute credit to the smiley waitress who patiently took orders in the middle of this, as there were about 10 different conversations going on at the same time with people randomly joining multiple discussions across tables. Mayhem.

3 very calm and demure people walked in wearing full Amy (Klobuchar) outfits to a rousing ovation of tongue-in-cheek applause and chants of 'Amy' 'Amy, Amy...'. It was done in a good spirit and they joined in with their kidnapped chant and had a laugh. They even chose to sit close to us in a massive restaurant with plenty of empty sections. The atmosphere reminded me of my university days living at a residential college that competed against rival colleges in sport and other endeavours. There was a spirit of jovial heckling that was fun to be involved in.

I devoured an avocado wrap - a token-healthy attempt that failed as it came surrounded by an American-sized portion of glistening chips (fries). I'd realised that I hadn't eaten since some service station (gas station) rubbish on the road from Cedar Rapids half a day ago. Bacon and eggs were being demolished all around me. By now it was around 4am, and I still hadn't given judicious thought to my exact plans. I learned that my Philly team were dropping off their hire car at the airport at about 5 and jumping onto flights home, booked for 6am. I'd been thinking that I'd check out a bit more of the Midwest on a bus back to Chicago, have a quick look around the windy city, and then keep on bussin' through the rust belt and trundle on into New England to pitch camp again.

'Fuck it. I'll come to the airport with you. May as well get myself straight over to New Hampshire to keep the show rolling.'

Change of plan.

It was the right decision. It was gonna take Greyhound a couple of days to relocate me, and I'd built up a head of campaigning steam that I didn't want to dissipate. So availing myself of some time with the splendidly discourteous staff of Delta Airlines was looming. That was my previous experience of flying domestic in the US, anyway. I was used to the perfectly groomed, smiling and attentive staff of the fine airlines of Asia. Their air hosts and hostesses, or flight attendants - ah, sorry, I believe cabin crew is now the PC-approved language - were charming, polite, and accommodating. Patient, sweet, helpful, and an all-round delight.

A far cry from the angst-ridden lot, seemingly reluctant to be of any real assistance, that I'd encountered on previous intra-US air travel. Simple requests were met with looks somewhat like a hungover father might give a teenage child when being pestered to listen to a new favourite pop song; that 'Get away from me with your poorly-timed request' look of scrunched up facial disdain not worth dignifying with words.

I hadn't slept for about a day, though, so couldn't imagine myself hitting them up with too many demanding requests.

I almost immediately gave up on trying to book through my phone, as we were very shortly to be airport-bound anyway and it would be easier face-to-face. The fine folks from Philadelphia had all pre-checked in and only had carry-on luggage, so we bade each other surprisingly fond farewells, considering we'd first met just the afternoon before, and I joined the check-in queue to make my enquiries.

I assume it was a fair bit busier than usual for a smallish Midwestern regional airport at 5am on a Tuesday morning. There were not many seats available to go anywhere, and I was correct in guessing that New Hampshire was a popular follow-on destination for the congregated political junkies. Boston would be fine and I could partially fulfil my original plan to bus it into the next-to-vote state in the absurdly long primary season.

'Nope, no availability to Boston, either, I'm afraid.'

'Ah, bugger. Ok.'

'Wait. If you don't mind going through Philly, I can connect you through to Boston from there.'

I was whistling with satisfaction as I wandered through to un-farewell my new friends to share a final little expedition in their commendable company.

We dosed up on coffee from a vat manned by an employee of a lucrative-minded airport café, which had set up a table for walk-through caffeine service in the bottle-neck that all travellers had to pass through before dispersing to their respective gates. A doughnut came as part of a reasonably priced combo that was taken up, as far as I could tell, by every weary soul about to jam into waiting lounges. I gobbled up my doughnut and guzzled down the coffee. I'm pretty sure I went back and did the same again, but I was in a bit of a daze until the ensuing sugar and caffeine rush kicked in, so I can't be sure. I went from zombie mode back to almost civilised alertness as newly-buzzed conversations about the caucus debacle restarted.

Chatting to one of the DSA guys - a confident, witty lad that had been at the coalface of the evening's antics - I realised that behind him, close enough to casually place a hand on his shoulder, was Jake Tapper, the CNN dude. He was so close that to verbalise this fact would have almost definitely been overheard, so I tried to pull off one of those take-a-look-behind-you half-pointing gestures with the corresponding eye-roll and head tilt. I also tried to also intimate an understated don't-try-to-do-it-too-emphatically-or-you'll-make-a-jackass-out-of-yourself-as-he's-less-than-half-a-metre-away-from-you vibe. Tough to pull off.

'You got a nervous tic or something, man?'

Not wanting to follow up with an awkward self-muffled voice or schoolkid whisper, I just said with about the same volume and tone as our existing chat,

'I believe that's Jake Tapper, the CNN fella, right behind you.'

'Ah, right. So it is.'

Jake may well have heard, but he continued half-chatting to a producer or, at least, one of the very few other soon-to-be passengers who was smartly attired in business casual.

I'd been trying to find a power socket that my international adaptor wouldn't fall out of. No matter what kind of bag, book or MacGyvered contraption I devised to prop it up, efforts to hold it in place had been futile. I wouldn't be beaten, though, as I knew that solo life on the road without a functioning phone would be ambitious.

With the kind assistance of another newly familiar face, I found a power source that allowed my phone to balance in place. Then ambling back to pick up where I'd left off my briefly interrupted chinwag, my prior companion was standing and having what looked to be a very engaging chat with Monsieur Tapper. As casually as I could muster with 2 (I believe) American-airport sized coffees, i.e. buckets, coursing through my veins, I joined them. My mate was saying,

'What a mess?'

'Yeah, really quite an embarrassing screw-up by the DNC and all involved,' Jake rejoined.

'Did you hear that the Buttigieg team has pretty strong connections with the Shadow Inc. company that's at the heart of this fiasco?', one of us offered.

'Yeah, it's pretty troubling.'

I did watch quite a bit of the very same Senor Tapper speaking at length about the failings of the Iowa caucus on TV the next night, but no-one asked him about the origins of Shadow Inc. He failed to bring it up himself, despite chatting rather knowledgeably about this highly topical point with a couple of random lads at an airport that very same morning. He spoke about it in quite some detail when pressed on the subject by us - questions that the panel of CNN experts didn't deem appropriate, it seemed.

A very smart guy, Jake; well-spoken, ultra-informed, and extremely professional. But he wasn't representing himself and the full range of his personal awareness and opinions on his mega rich cable network. Rather, he gave voice to views laid out in pre-show editorial meetings or more likely ones just inherently understood as being within the boundaries of what's acceptable to discuss in order to keep the billionaire network owners satisfied with the incredibly well-paid job that he does.

Chris Hayes on MSNBC occasionally throws a very progressive bone out there on his Twitter feed, usually when coming under fire from online suggestions that he has transformed himself into a corporate lackey. My initial instinct when I see examples of his scant 'gifts' to the true left is to be impressed by him calling it straight and giving dues to people who are trying to represent the public's interests. But then I remember that he consciously embraces a company-endorsed attitudinal compromise on TV, that perhaps overrides his true beliefs, in order to continue receiving lavish paychecks. He opts to represent the views of his overlords for great personal financial gain, and thus my admiration for him hastily loses its shine.

These media paradigm setters are not 'fake news' or conspiracy theorists. It's just that choosing what to focus on and what to omit from the conversation is essential in setting the boundaries of the narrative, simply reflecting their role as corporate mouthpieces programmed to maintain the status quo for their owner's financial interests. When it comes to reporting on food, travel, the Arts, culture etc there is no finer journalistic excellence to be found, but on economic or military issues there is an unwritten, rarely spoken, requirement not to rock the boat, which is sailing through bounteous waters (often at someone else's expense), for their gilded captains at the helm of this exploitative opulence.

Alrighty then, back in the Des Moines airport waiting area, I also spied Matt Taibbi (again) minding his own business with headphones in and iPad out. I saw a couple of our gang also doing some fangirling when they spotted him. I realised that I'd finished reading his newest book, Hate Inc., just before jetting out of Korea, so sadly didn't have it with me, as it was beckoning for his signature. I did cart over a couple of books which were in similar need of marking by their esteemed authors, though.

'On Fire', by my 2nd favourite political writer (behind Chomsky), the brilliant and thorough Naomi Klein, was top of my list. She was a Sanders surrogate and I thought there'd be a good chance of running into her. As it happened, in all my wading into political fanzones, NK never crossed my path to grace her pages with her name in ink.

Another one was 'The Chapo Guide to Revolution', collaboratively written by the comedic political podcast team, 'Chapo Traphouse'. Those guys are funny, and impressively well-informed, and I'd booked in for one of their shows in NH, so was a fair chance to get pen to paper from some of them.

I should have realised that MT would have been around, too. Schoolboy error.

His political commentary is astute and entertaining. He's worked for Rolling Stone for years and I've heard him and others refer to his fondness for the Gonzo writing style of Hunter S. Thomson. I'm sure Matt would be doing the scattered dust of Hunter proud. He's an impressive journalist and gifted writer. I wanted to let him know how much I'd appreciated reading his gems for years, and to shake his hand. But I didn't want to be an obtrusive dick about it, so I was as espionage-focused as I could be - keeping an eye on him until that golden moment when he'd get up to board and wander over towards the gate.

A couple of others had the same intention and as the boarding announcement rang out, 3 of us descended into his presence in a similar faux-casual way as I had with Tapper, J., just before. The 2 lasses got a photo with him, and he was taken aback by the attention and warmly appreciative – such an easy-going, literally approachable guy. My moment was up,

> 'Hi, Matt. I just wanted to say how much I've enjoyed reading your insightful, informative, and entertaining writing for many years now. I've just finished reading 'War Inc.'. and it nails the current polarised nature of US media. Loved it. Thanks so much and keep up your great work.'

> 'Oh, gee. Thanks,' came his natural reply.

I'd gone over my mini-spiel in my head a few times and just about got it bang on, other than the fact that I'm pretty sure I got the name of his book wrong. 'War Inc.' is a movie by Armando Iannucci, satirising the lunacy of war, whereas his book is 'Hate Inc.', which expertly lampoons the deliberately-divisive, over-ly-sensationalised, factional folly of legacy media. He must have noticed, but perhaps didn't mind so much, as I'd suggest his title was chosen well-armed with this knowledge and perhaps even as a little homage to Iannucci's brilliant work.

Iannucci's 'The Thick of It' is a masterpiece of political satire, as if 'Yes, Minister' (and 'Yes, Prime Minister') had been re-writ-ten with the same sharp political observations, but spiced up by the obscenity-laced ghost of Richard Pryor and the fleshy con-tributions of Larry David's superb, semi-improvised situational humour.

The US spin-off, 'Veep', is also great, with Elaine Benice showing her expert proliferation for cussing. However, it still pales in comparison to the most recent Scottish Dr. Who, playing Malcolm Tucker in 'The Thick of It', who is the definitive 'cusser-in-chief'. Surely he is the best swearer in the history of television, although the aptly-named Al Swearingen from 'Deadwood' gives him a good run.

We Aussies are pretty good at our creative dedication to potty-mouthedness, but I ruefully admit that I think the Scots have got us licked. Nothing sounds as effortlessly foul, yet innately fitting, as a diatribe of lewd offensiveness spewed forth with a thick Celtic burr from a Scotsman, possibly named Big Jock McFilth, or a wee bonnie lassie who could tear strips off men twice her size with a tirade of defiling indecency that would make Mel Gibson blush.

The coffee wore off as the double-legged trip panned out with bleary, mumbled conversations and a repeat farewell with the Philly crew, comprising weary, yet enthusiastic, hugs and heartfelt well wishes. Both hops were pretty short, but I got in about 10-15 minutes of semi-meaningful discussion with the NBC Boston cameraman I sat next to during the first leg (before we both fell into a brief half-doze), who I followed as he led me along the transfer route he knew well enough to complete on sleep-deprived auto-pilot, saving me from thinking, which my primitive brain capacity at that time appreciated.

Baahston airport had the same glistening newness as Chicago's. I began relishing the imagined feeling that I'd landed in the middle of a story-building scene from 'The Town', 'The Departed', or 'Black Mass'. I wasn't too keen to be involved in the next scene, though, where a body was sure to be stashed in the back of a car, as my cinematic experiences with such thick local accents suggested was inevitable.

It was starting to seem that being a natural entertainer is a pre-requisite to drive interstate buses in the US. This next lad, tasked with safely conveying us into The Granite State from the capital of Massachusetts, was also full of wise-cracks and quips. Using careful, yet barely constrained, PC language, he had perfected his opening comedy routine about what would happen to us if we got grossly inebriated (he definitely wanted to say 'shit-faced') on the bus mid-trip and urinated (pissed) all over the seat of the latrine (crapper) at the back.

Leaning back in our comfortable seats, the recently-landed patrons didn't seem to be in great need of this advice, more suited to a group of uni students intent on warming up on their post-exam trip up to a friend's cabin. This partially filled airport bus contained snappily-dressed businesspeople, older folks no doubt off to visit kids and grandkids, and an extremely tired, but mostly well-behaved Aussie who was unnaturally wide-eyed - the desperate backlash of a body trying to stave off strengthening symptoms of sleep deprivation. He was peering out the window trying to figure out at which end of a cinematographically recognised bridge Southies lived. It should have been easier than it was proving to be for his drowsy, frazzled mind.

This 2nd bus trip on my 2020 expedition also turned out to be genteel and pleasant, unlike my nightmarish memories of trips using Greyhound buses in the US over scattered journeys past where I alertly stayed awake and at the ready to ensure that I wasn't robbed, stabbed or molested. The limited number of times I'd waited at downtown bus depots stateside all made the wretched hive of scum and villainy of the Cantina Bar, along with the vampire-infested one in 'From Dusk Til Dawn', look tame - full of deadbeats, druggos, dropouts, the destitute and desperate.

When about to climb aboard a late-night bus from NY to DC a few years back, I was sure that one fella had a shotgun inside his trenchcoat and was eyeing me off to take down first, so I was ever-prepared to dive for cover before getting to the relative safety of my seat. If you want to see the bottom end of a struggling society, going to the hubs of the nation's cheapest long-distance public transport system is a pretty good place to start.

I finally solved my simple mental query to locate South Boston, where Whitey Bulger made a name for himself. This was also the region Matt Damon (said with 'Team America: World Police' pronunciation), the brothers Affleck, Mork, that young dude from 'Titanic', the guy from 'The Shining' that you wouldn't want to share home isolation with, and Edward Scissorhands, must have all hung out to perfect the hard-edged, street-tough, working-class accent for their respective Southie roles.

It must've been easier for Private Ryan and the guy from Pearl Harbor, as they grew up just on the other side of the recently referenced bridge, which was the physical manifestation of the class divide that it represented. While prepping up for their break-out film, they presumably brought Mrs. Doubtfire along to get in the same linguistic swing, spending time becoming familiar with the regional peccadillos of locals from this rough region. Southies weren't that far geographically from Harvard or MIT, although I don't think that was the standard pathway for most from this notorious neighbourhood.

My sleep cycles were all over the place and, in my over-alert state of bodily overcompensation, I decided to try to ride it out until I could crash upon setting myself up in my hotel, New Hampshire (apologies for the weak, thoroughly avoidable, John Irving reference).

I'd always heard that the countryside is beautiful up there and I wasn't disappointed; verdant green fields, tall, leafy trees – or, to be more botanically accurate, the 'mixed oaks of the Northeastern coastal forests' (thanks, Wikipedia) – were being showcased as we motored north towards the upper end of the Appalachians.

New England seemed appropriately named at this moment, as it appeared cleaner and fresher than ye olde England, and so far hadn't revealed unwashed masses with yellow teeth.

I was actually born in London before being transported to Aus after a few dreary months, no doubt for some minor theft as was the traditional path. This is my flimsy justification for such an uncalled-for sleight against our fine mother-country cousins – like comedians of a certain identity wading in with gratuitous, un-PC routines against their own that would demand court appearances if done by other non-identity-aligned contemporaries.

I offer a non-humble half-apology to all my loosely-associated fellow poms.

Manchester is a picturesque and productive town; just that right size – having everything you could ask for, while also not being too in-your-face. Straddling the impressive Merrimack River, once home to a thriving paper-production industry, it had now revamped itself into an innovative tech hub, with spacious offices set up in refitted former riverside mills.

The leviathan of online learning; University of Southern New Hampshire, is also situated here, which was one of the deciding factors for me choosing this particular town to base myself in. I'd done a post-grad degree in US Political Science by correspondence through them a few years back (topped the course!) and felt an affinity and curiosity to check it out. My already positive feelings about the place were heightened as soon as I jumped out of my transport smack bang in the middle of town. Spending an invigorating 10 minutes or so wandering over to the nearest bridge to take it all in, the cool air and amiable surroundings helped ward off my encroaching sleepiness.

My older brother, Drew, dialled in from Oz at this well-timed moment of contented absorption,

'Happy Birthday, mate!'

'Really, still?'

'Yeah, got a few hours to go.'

'Is that right? Thought that finished days ago. Thanks.'

'No worries. Where are ya?'

'Just got into New Hampshire. Exactly where I wanna be.'

'Nice one. How is it?'

'Lovely, but cold.'

Iowa was chilly - this was a significant 5 to 10 degrees cooler. A feat not easily achieved. Bracing.

I'd used my well-charged phone to book what I was later told was one of the last hotel rooms available in town, now finding out that it was but a short walk upstream along the riverside. I would walk as briskly as the weather, and was happy to do so.

On the way, I spotted a small building that seemed a little unkempt and run-down. I didn't investigate too closely, but it looked like the sort of derelict abode that squatters could target as a ramshackle roof over their heads to avoid over-exposure to these frigid conditions.

This was the Biden campaign headquarters in Manchester. There was a flimsy forest of flagging signs that stood very un-proudly outside, wedged thoughtlessly into the snowy approaches. At this time, this seemed reflective of the Biden campaign - kind of shabby. Looked like the lights were on, but nobody was home. Hopefully that doesn't prove to be too predictive for Uncle Joe.

I rolled on, crossed a bridge further down, and sauntered into the very accommodating La Quinta Inn, overlooking the wid-est part of the mighty Merrimack, in this urban zone, at least. I choose to name this place, as it was clean, well-run, and fairly priced. It was only 1 more listed star than my Cedar Rapids haunt, but was in a whole different galaxy, light years ahead, in terms of its facilities, operation, and service.

Exactly what my flagging body needed - a cosy room with re-liable hot water, a heater that wasn't having a mental breakdown, a big flat-screen TV, and soft, inviting sheets.

It had been a long day.

E. Mini-rant 5 – Media for the People

I have immense respect for people who rose up through journalistic ranks due to their dedication and talent, making it to a level where certain compromises to their 'voice' were required, and they then refused to sell out their genuine beliefs and concerns for what they believed in.

I'm talking here about Krystal Ball (yes, a silly name, but a seriously noteworthy journalist), who worked at MSNBC but got spat out for her refusal to buckle to network demands. She now co-hosts the excellent 'The Hill Rising' YouTube channel with Saagar Engeti, who provides a bit of balance with his somewhat more right-leaning views on social and cultural issues, but who shows the vast overlap between 'left' and 'right' when it comes to shared economic (and military) concerns. He is always thoughtful and informative, also, as they add their valuable voices to the public forum. Please check them out; they provide vital insights across the spectrum of US politics. This is one prominent example of the kind of New Media that is breaking free of the corporate shackles, yet is presented in a slick, professional manner.

Cenk Uygur, the founder of the The Young Turks, went down the same path, which he documents in a YouTube clip explaining how, after filling in for Ed Schultz on MSNBC and attaining noticeably high ratings, he was 'called upstairs' and given a talking to. He was offered a sizeable pay rise to pull back on his balanced analysis of the Democratic administration because it was making them look bad.

'As a result of exposure on the Air America radio network, MSNBC hired Uygur[5] as a contributor and substitute anchor for the network on October 21, 2010. On January 21,

2011, Uygur was made the host of the 6 p.m. Eastern slot on MSNBC as the anchor of a new prime time edition of MSNBC Live, after the network parted ways with Keith Olbermann, resulting in a rearrangement of the time slots of MSNBC's other prime time shows. Uygur filled the time slot vacated by Ed Schultz,[44][45] from late January through June 2011, earning first among people 18–34 in the second quarter.

Management saw the style of several hosts, including Uygur, as off base from MSNBC's branding objectives that resulted in their demotion.[46] According to Uygur, Phil Griffin, the President of MSNBC disliked his "aggressive style" and told him the network's audience "require different manners of speaking".[46] MSNBC denied Uygur's statements that the network desired censorship of his anti-corporate stances and both sides agreed that their main differences of opinion were about the style of communication.[46] His contract was ended when he was offered to move to weekend slot, but declined.[46][7][47] After leaving cable news, Uygur devoted his attention to TYT.[46] Uygur over time became disillusioned with traditional media establishments.[6]' (Wikipedia)

YouTube: Cenk Uygur on Democracy Now! About Leaving MSNBC After Being Told to "Act Like An Insider"

There is a brilliant show on Australia's government-run channel, ABC (Australian Broadcasting Corporation), called 'Media Watch', which provides critical examinations of how different media decisions are made and why. It should be compulsory viewing for all Australians, in the same way that Democracy Now! should be for Americans, in my opinion.

Ed Schultz (RIP) himself tried to film his show live from the launch of the Sanders campaign, but when pushing back against editorial decisions not to cover the kick-off of the only other viable campaign against Hillary Clinton in 2015, he received a call directly from Phil Griffin, MSNBC's CEO, to unequivocally, according to Schultz, instruct him to drop the story. Here's the relevant entry in Wikipedia,

'In an interview with National Review's Jamie Weinstein[note 1] Schultz stated that he had prepared a report on Bernie Sanders' presidential candidate announcement at his home, but five minutes before the broadcast was due to air, he was angrily told by then-president of MSNBC Phil Griffin that "you're not covering this" and "you're not covering Bernie Sanders".[44][45]

Schultz stated that he objected to the prohibition because he felt the topic of a presidential candidate announcement was relevant, but was told not to cover the announcement, and that he would be covering press conferences in Texas and Baltimore which had already been outlined, which Schultz referred to as "totally meaningless".[44]

Schultz stated that he felt the reason for the termination 45 days after the Sanders announcement was because Hillary Clinton and Andrew Lack were "joined at the hip", and that MSNBC was "in the tank with Hillary Clinton", that the process was managed by executives, who did not want their primetime hosts affiliating with anyone other than Hillary Clinton.[44][45]

Schultz also stated that after being hired as a host for RT America, that he had more creative freedom and was not dictated to with regard to editorial content, and that he was doing "real journalism" at RT, as opposed to MSNBC, which he characterized as "opinion".'

Back in the early years of the new millennium, Phil Donahue continually critiqued the Iraq War, commenting on its unjustified beginning and destructive results – his flagship talk show was canned. And this was also on MSNBC, a supposedly liberal network.

'In July 2002, Phil Donahue returned to television after seven years of retirement to host a show called Donahue on MSNBC.[19] On February 25, 2003, MSNBC canceled the show.[20][21]

Soon after the show's cancellation, an internal MSNBC memo was leaked to the press stating that Donahue should be fired because he opposed the imminent U.S. invasion of Iraq and that he would be a "difficult public face for NBC in a time of war" [22] and that his program could be "a home for the liberal anti-war agenda".[23] Donahue commented in 2007 that the management of MSNBC, owned at the time by General Electric, a major defense contractor, required that "we have two conservative (guests) for every liberal. I was counted as two liberals."[24]' (Wikipedia)

You can only get to high-ranking, journalistic talking head positions if you tow the party line. Of course, that's how the corporate world works. Unless you're a loyal company player, i.e. a 'Yes Man/ Woman', you're not gonna get anywhere near the top of a show.

The Pulitzer Prize-winning former NY Times writer, Chris Hedges, is another good example of an ethical investigative reporter whose career path was diverted by sycophantic-to-power editorial decree around the time of the Iraq War.

'Hedges was an early critic of the Iraq War. In May 2003, he delivered a commencement address at Rockford College in Rockford, Illinois, saying: "We are embarking on an occupation that, if history is any guide, will be as damaging to our souls as it will be to our prestige and power and security."[27] His speech was received with boos and his microphone was shut off three minutes after he began speaking.[28]

The New York Times, his employer, criticized his statements and issued him a formal reprimand for "public remarks that could undermine public trust in the paper's impartiality".[29] Shortly after the incident, Hedges left The New York Times to become a senior fellow at The Nation Institute, and a columnist at Truthdig, in addition to writing books and teaching inmates at a New Jersey correctional institution.[29][30]' (Wikipedia)

Also, a huge shout-out here to:

Kyle Kulinski – Secular Talk.

Mike Figueredo – The Humanist Report.

David Doel – The Rational National.

I don't know much about the background stories of these excellent political YouTube commentators, but I do know that they bring everyday awareness about the political realities of the US system through a focused lens of un-corporatised analysis.

2.

NHP minus 5: We're Not Here to Fuck Spiders

Well rested, I was up early to maximise my intake at the well-stocked breakfast buffet. It offered stodgy fare galore to help build up some extra insulation against the biting conditions outside. A waffle maker proudly stood in one corner, the fine art of which I needed a few mild pointers (it's all about a well-timed flip); pro-tips that I was passing on to new arrivals in days ahead like an expert in waffle-making machinations. A pancake maker was just diagonally opposite it (kitty or catty corner for some Americans reading this; expressions which I've heard many times from North American co-workers, which never fail to bring a smile to my mug). This was a little easier to operate; it involved pressing the button that, had space permitted, would have had written on it,

> 'Push here for everything required for me to make you the pancake of your dreams; perfectly-mixed batter deposition onto a carefully-timed, top-and-bottom heated conveyance with smooth discharge at the completion of my

masterful self-operating assembly line - just don't forgot to put a plate under the end of the conveyor belt where I will plonk your impeccably-produced pancake perfection ready for you to feast upon.'

So, you could stand in this corner of the smorgasbord and simultaneously line up a voluminous quadrant of dual (perhaps duelling) morning carbs. Betwixt this overload of energy was the corner of condiments; super-sugary, hyper-whipped cream, about as light and fluffy as a childish imagining of clouds, a melody of nuts and raisins for sprinkling, as well as a radioactive blueberry goo, which was as viscous as honey that had been put in the fridge.

I was hungry, so piled a Himalayan range of these offerings onto numerous garbage-can-lid-sized (trash can, in US vernacular) plates and availed myself of the bottomless pots of coffee, energetically refilled by dutiful and attentive kitchen staff, kept busy by the ravenous hordes. Plenty were up early in the recently sold-out hotel, with some incongruous Aussie-out-of-water (like a fish) perhaps having slotted into the final gap.

On this first morning's assault, I aimed to sample at least a little from each of the assembled availabilities. So I went back more times than I'd like to share with you to sample muffins, Danish pastries, little tubs of yoghurt, buns and breads to toast, and much more generously portioned mini peel-back tubs of peanut butter and jam (jelly) than in my Iowan dump of a hotel. Actually, there were multiple fruity conserves, ready to be blended with those moreish cream cheese solo sachet servings that are scrumptious with a dark jam on top of an English muffin.

I was making an absolute pig of myself.

There was comfortable seating at roomy tables, as well as couches on which to take a well-earned breather before heading back into the fray. All set up within eyeshot of a large TV updating everyone interested in the mainstream take on the previous days political news and predictions of what was to come. I was there early and stayed 'til near the end of the designated a.m. banquet hours. In a desperate last-ditch grasp for salubrity, I grabbed a take-away apple (to go) as I repaired back to my room to kit up for the day's onslaught ahead.

I called reception to book a cab and wandered down to wait in the foyer (lobby) to find further treats, left ungobbled by the seemingly insatiable breakfasters, now looking inviting next to a chilled lemon water dispenser, an abundance of coffee, and complimentary papers. I could easily have found myself a garish smoking jacket with a matching pair of felt-lined slippers and settled in for the day. But there were bigger fish to fry out there, so I was eager, but sluggish, to set forth upon hearing the local cabbie's arrival beep.

Trying to put my seat belt into its slot, I fumbled around unsuccessfully for long enough to feel quite awkward and a little flummoxed. What was wrong with me that I couldn't complete my day's first and surely one of its simplest tasks?

'Ah, it's got a protector thing in there so it doesn't beep at me if someone doesn't wanna put their belt on,' finally came the grizzled voice of the swarthy, unshaven chap in the driver's seat.

'Oh, strange. I've never seen one of those before,' as he ejected a cordless metal belt buckle out of my socket and tossed it into the glovebox in front of me.

'There ya go, if you wanna belt up.'

'Don't you have to these days?'

'Not in New Hampshire. No seat belt law.'

'Really?'

'Yep, Live free or die.'

I remembered that this was their state motto, and not just this fella's cavalier, libertarian approach to life... and death. But I didn't realise there was such practical potential to prove it. Rather than live free AND die, I decided to,

'Live temporarily restrained and try to reduce the percentage chances of an early demise,' and strapped myself in.

Call me a pussy, if you like.

Bill Bryson, the magnificent travel writer, who lived in these parts for a while, comments on this very matter in 'I'm a Stranger

Here Myself: Notes on Returning to America After 20 Years Away' by stating,

> 'Still I can't criticize because I live in the state with the most demented of all license plate slogans, the strange and pugnacious "Live Free or Die". Perhaps I take these things too literally, but I really don't like driving around with an explicit written vow if things don't go right. Frankly, I would prefer something a little more equivocal and less terminal – "Live Free or Pout" perhaps, or maybe "Live Free or Bitch Mightily to Anyone Who'll Listen"'

I engaged in some chit-chat with this barely intelligible chap who had a bit of that Irish brogue that I was familiar with from other non-Irish, having spent quite a bit of time with the fine folks of Newfoundland, who seem to frequent the shores of Korea in greater percentages than their number should suggest. I focused hard to try to catch what he was saying, as he mumbled through the permanent cigarette hanging out of the side of his mouth in his beaten up old taxi that appeared not to have been cleaned, inside or out, for decades. Food containers and random flotsam and jetsam were strewn all through the back seat and on the floor. I was thankfully sitting in the passenger seat, but neither was it a Marie Kondo-inspired minimalist's delight.

I was curious to get his take on matters political and tried to casually steer the jumbled discussion onto matters pertinent to the approaching primary, but he barely seemed to know that it was happening and showed zero humanly recognisable signs of interest or knowledge.

I'd almost forgotten that there are radio stations still sticking it out with hits purely from the 60s, 70s, and 80s and I was fondly tapping away to tunes I hadn't heard in years as I reminisced about the world that I believe this chap was still living in. He mumbled along in a gruff, unmelodic monotone with words to REO Speedwagon, and others powerhouses of that ilk, that I wouldn't have been able to distinguish if it wasn't for the fact that I could also hear the original tune sung with both melody and comprehensible enunciation.

He grunted an unknown farewell to me as I gave a generous tip due to the fact that I found his company to be entertainingly undecipherable and also because I hated having too many notes or especially coins (he didn't have a credit card option). When forced to pay cash, I'd always try to round up to the nearest decent decimal denomination. He thanked me. I think.

My imminent entry into another Bernie branch brought a joy to my heart, so I set foot inside with expectant optimism. Again there was an energy in the room, which was laid out in battle-ready mode - this was a very active hub. There was a check-in desk upon entry, tables of organisers flanking one side of the room in a long row, and a post-canvassing table set up both to gather relevant voter information and return unused 'lit'(erature): campaign handouts, flyers etc, which I'd been using almost long enough to justify using the campaign abbreviation for - like 'merch' for campaign products that were on sale. I should have been good at sliding into such terminology as an Aussie with in-herent abbreviating tendencies, but always treaded carefully when introducing new terms into my daily linguistic usage to avoid looking like a try-hard wanker. Pretty soon, however, I would be,

'Here's my extra lit'-ing.

And

'Any good new merch?'-ifying at will, but only around those who I knew to be fully on board with such jargon.

I checked in with a trustingly added signature on a required volunteer form (hope I didn't agree to sell my soul to Bernie, although I'd trust him with it a lot more than most) and a quick iPad info entry, with a fictitious US phone number added for necessity along with 90210 – my lone go-to to satisfy postcode (zip code) needs. Then I headed over to the row of officials to get my marching orders. No, not like that - my turf to cruise around with an online list of doors to knock on.

'Ah, you're an Aussie,' still pronounced like 'posse'.

'Yep.'

A really warm and welcoming chat followed where I told these guys that I was fully at their disposal for the next 6 or 7 days, and made a point of having a quick chat to each of the half dozen team leaders – Will, Kate, Lety, Nick, Sus, and James - who were gonna be the lifeblood of this centre during the weekly countdown to go-time. They were a well-oiled operation with a friendly atmosphere of collective effort and shared intent. And, importantly when you are in each other's company day-in, day-out for months on end, they were not only very tight and team-oriented, but also fun to be around,

'Alright, well we're not here to fuck spiders.'

'What's that?', came my puzzled response.

'We're not here to fuck spiders.'

'Ah, nope. That's certainly true.'

I picked up on the gist of the 'time to get to work' motivational intent of the arachnid-lovin' statement and had, perhaps, heard it before, but it didn't ring a loud bell. I looked it up on Urban Dictionary later, keen to learn the origin of the distinctively Aussie phrase, but only got examples of usage and meaning, which I'd pretty much gathered already. It did proffer an alternative PC version, though, which caught my attention,

'We're not here to fornicate with arachnids.'

Someone's creative and perhaps chemically-stimulated mind came up with this. Not bad.

'We're not here for a fucking haircut,' was the closest equivalent that sprang to mind, with a similar inspirational message of,

'Enough chit-chat; time to get down to business.'

I'd heard the haircut version, which reflects a more amorous intent, as a teenager when uttered by pimply youngsters trying to convey the sort of false Cassanova-esque confidence to their mates that suggested that they were about to show well-honed, magnetic, lady-luring skills, before bumbling over to the unfortunate recipient of their awkward, voice-breaking incompetence as they tripped over both their words and feet.

I was less familiar with the 8-legged version, however, but realised it was more focused on inspiring action in general.

'Have you met Alistair?'

'No, I don't think so.'

'He's our resident Aussie. He's been teaching us some of your slang.'

'If he's got any more spider shaggin' Aussie-isms, he might have to enlighten me, too,' I thought, but didn't verbalise, as I didn't want to lose any of the polish off my over-esteemed Aussie schtick.

We were introduced.

'How are ya, mate?'

'Yeah, good, eh.'

'How long ya bin up this way?'

'Oh, yeah. You know. A bit now. She's pretty chilly out, but ya harden up pretty quick smart, eh. Gotta take a concrete pill or bugger off, I reckon.'

'Yeah, blood oath, mate.'

It wasn't quite this ocker (which Wikipedia describes as, 'an Australian who speaks and acts in a rough and uncultivated manner, using a broad Australian accent') but there is a little tendency I've noticed when chancing upon another random Aussie in a foreign land to 'Aussie it up' a bit, and we were both, rather enjoyably, displaying this in our greeting.

He's an outstanding lad. Previously based in New York, he'd now been with the campaign in New Hampshire for a good few months. It was refreshing to meet another die-hard Berner from the same southern shores. There's an article in The Guardian detailing Alistair's involvement in the campaign as an Aussie, along with another bloke, also called Alistair (I was breaking this trend as a non-Alistair Aussie US-political tragic). He asked if I'd mind also being contacted for this article and I readily consented, but never got the call up. Here's some insight into the Aussie Alistairs' commendable contributions to American political activism,

---

Google: The Guardian Primary school:
the Australians volunteering in Democratic campaigns

Still in Manchester's thriving field office, I hooked up with Frank, a champion fella up from Connecticut, who had wheels and was happy to have a partner in crime. We were assigned a cluster of houses in a scenic little community about a half hour out of town. It was a glorious day for a drive and a walk in the crisp, fresh air. So we thanked the team for the info and, on our way out, I offered a token throwaway farewell along the lines of 'Thanks and see you a bit later then',

'Cheers,' I said wandering towards the door.

'Cheers,' came the first reply.

'Yep, cheers,' chimed in another.

'Cheers,' echoed a third.

Then a 4th and a 5th...

More 'cheers' than a Christmas drinking session continued to rain down. This was something else the regulars had picked up from Alistair and they were delighting in the opportunity to show off their newfound material with tongue-in-cheek revelry on an unsuspecting recipient. Excellent stuff.

It was reminiscent of that scene out of 'Spies Like Us' –

'Doctor, doctor... doctor'.

There's a little homage to this in the more recent 'Jojo Rabbit' with a scene dedicated to 'Heil Hitler' hi's and bye's.

Frank was a musician and played me some of his stuff on the trip. Really good. He was also the spitting image of Adam Driver, and when I enquired whether as a single lad this fact was of any benefit with female fans of Kylo Ren, he said,

'I don't just go out for a fucking haircut.'

Nah, not really. He rather demurely suggested that it hadn't done him any harm on a few occasions. He shouldn't get a haircut either, otherwise the Driver doppelgängery would suffer a little.

Despite his ways with the force, he was less familiar with knocking on doors, well for political purposes, anyway. I was no veteran, but took the lead role early on. He was a wise young Jedi master, though, so we quickly fell into a natural rhythm of taking turns as the lead with the other playing a strong supporting role. In hindsight, he should have used more Jedi mind tricks on the weak-minded,

'Bloomberg's not the candidate you're looking for. He can go back to his business. Move him along.'

Bugger. Next time.

There was often a bit of driving required to link between sections of this well-forested, semi-rural township next to a sizeable lake. We developed a little game (continued with others as the week rolled on) where we'd predict the political inclination of the face behind the next door based on the demographic indicators provided. We got pretty good at it -

William Stephenson, 72.

'Biden.'

'Yep.'

Isabella Martinez, 22.

'Bernie.'

'Right.'

Mary Masters, 53.

'Liz.'

'No.'

'Pete.'

'Nup, Amy.'

'Ah, really? Damn it.'

Jamie Williams, 39.

'Ah, hang on. Tough one. Not sure.'

Obviously, age was key. Names weren't so helpful here, in such a predominantly white community. But the state of a house, of course, reflected the general level of affluence or otherwise, which was a key determinative factor. Kids' play-stuff also indicated household dynamics. The type and number of vehicles in the drive, the standard of yard maintenance, and the general upkeep of the dwelling all played a role. Of course, as different runs were situated in differing socio-economic communities, the trends were often very region-specific, too.

Most doors were assigned to us with the ideal that a voter or voters within were likely or at least a chance of voting in the up-coming Democratic party primary. The info was far from perfect, though, and lots of Trump voters (quite possibly former Obama voters) lurked behind doors. In all honesty, the overwhelming vibe that I got from these folks was either staunch adherence to right-leaning political partisanship or a disgust with the system overall. Very high percentages of these people were polite, and willing to share their thoughts in a calm, rational manner.

I tried out a different strategy with a few Trumpers by ex-plaining that Sanders supporters, like them, were not big fans of the Democratic establishment. I suggested the no-lose situation of throwing in a vote for Bernie to stick it to Pelosi and co. (then go with Donnie-boy in the general, if they so desired). People agreed that there was some sense in this, but I'd be surprised if anyone actually took me up on my progressive grand bargain.

One clearly affluent household provided an interesting in-sight into these distorted dynamics. The most confident and charismatic mum engaged us on her doorstep and rejoiced in telling us she was a Trump voter. Her boy was a Bernie fan, she told us,

'Aren't you, Jimmy?'

'Yep, Bernie all the way.'

'Come and talk to us, Jimmy,' we gently implored.

'Can't. I'm in the middle of an important GTA mission.'

'Pause it, dude!'

'Nah!'

'You gonna vote?'

'Yeah, probably.'

'Will you be able to leave your game for long enough?'

'Yeah, I think so.'

'Do you boys wanna drink?' mum kindly offered.

'Sure. That'd be great, actually.'

'How about some apple juice poppers?'

'Perfect!'

'How's your mission going, Jimmy?' we enquired.

'I'm on fire!'

'Make sure you vote, dude.'

'Alright.'

'Ah, thank you so much. Truly interesting to talk to you both,' as we gratefully accepted the drinks.

'You, too, boys.'

'All the best.'

'See ya.'

'Cheers. Bye.'

We never saw Jimmy's face. Hope he voted. It's time for the Jimmy's of the world to get off the couch and get active.

The Aussie thing helped with Trumpers, too, as it was disarming to most that I'd turned up from a land most knew little about other than a media-fuelled obsession with how many things can kill you down there (in a land of cougars, bears, rattlesnakes, and scorpions).

Over countless discussions about deadly Aussie wildlife with people from far reaches of this big, blue marble (my wife and I ran a guesthouse in Seoul for about 6 years, so this was a regular occurrence), I waver between various approaches depending on my mood, the general atmosphere, and the predicted response of the target,

'It's getting much safer these days. I believe recent studies have shown that only about 8% (or maybe 3% for a wiser mark) of travellers to Australia suffer fatal or life-altering injuries from an animal attack these days...'

Or

'Snakes and spiders are the least of your worries. It's the little-known drop bears than cause the most damage. Gotta always be looking up when you're in the bush (forest). Koalas hang on tight, but drop bears can fall on you at any moment and they're heavy enough to... Well, it's not good.'

Or, boringly,

'You do realise that almost all Australians live in cities like yours and rarely have anything to do with wild animals other than the occasional stray cat. Those 'Australia: Home of the Most Vicious Killers of the Animal Kingdom' are hyped to the max because they are about an unknown land that can be made out to be a fantastical realm of fear and inevitable death at any moment to boost shock-fuelled ratings. If they chose to focus on North America, the footage they could dig up on bear attacks alone would dwarf anything that we can produce in the terror stakes.'

'Yes, but you've got nasty spiders and you can't see them coming.'

'They're not out to get you. If you see one, step on it. Take your pick: bear, cougar, or spider?'

Speaking of dangerous members of the animal kingdom, Adam Driver and I did pick the winner of the game show 'What Nutter is Behind that Door?', after cautiously wandering up to the entrance to one particular house on our run. Part of the demographic breakdown was seeing places that were, how should I say, run down as fuck. This screamed; single older male, no kids, unlikely to be holding a highly-paid job, but probably holding a shotgun.

We discussed skipping this place for these exact reasons, but were pretty close to it and maybe had some male pride kicking in. I was an Aussie raised in the 70s and 80s, and he was an international heartthrob. We couldn't show weakness.

We looked across at each other with mutual dread as we saw the doorbell, which we kinda now had to ring, or turn and scamper like pussies. The doorbell was surrounded by the most ornate part of the entire hovel, which doesn't say a great deal, to be fair. It was an intricate, purple skull-and-cross-bones, which flashed and played a demonic tune when pressed. Genuine warning signs.

He was mid-stride as the door flung open requiring us to jump in retreat, and he kept coming with a purposeful gait. I probably don't need to emphasise the fact that he chose a fiercely vitriolic tone, as I'd imagine his chosen words are rarely spoken with a light-hearted playfulness,

> 'Fucking communists. Get the fuck off my lawn,' as mentioned before, were his exact words, as they are etched into my mind, which was swiftly lifted into a heightened state.

It's not often you get that 'fight-or-flight' instinct kicking in. With no other option, I think I could embrace the requirement to fight, but flight was far and away my preference.

Scampering to the hopeful safety of the car, glancing with genuine concern over our shoulders to ensure buckshot wasn't chasing us, we were unnecessarily polite,

'Yes, certainly sir. Apologies for our intrusion. Very sorry to bother you. Have a nice day.'

This was a great example of the British instincts still present in American culture, despite all the brainwashing about exceptionalism. Someone can be uttering the rudest words that you've been subjected to, since your schoolyard days, and yet remorse is shown for having the bald-faced rudeness to turn up for a chat on their doorstep to preach inclusiveness and public assistance programs. The hide of some of us.

'Have a nice day' might have been overkill, but you do what's necessary when self-protection instincts take hold.

I've never really understood thrill-seekers who choose to put their life on the line to get a rush, but this brief burst of adrenaline offered a fleeting glimpse. It was alarming, but also kind of electrifying, to suddenly think that you might be shot at. Once my heart rate was down again, though, I decided that it was an experience that I didn't want to become commonplace.

We eventually retreated to the safety of the 'house of cheers' and checked in with recommened jovial chats and the anecdote about our little encounter with living proof that redbaiting works. He was no doubt enflamed by countless hours of solitary inculcation from paranoia-provoking, anger-stoking Fox News snake-oil salesmen and women. As Yoda said,

'Fear is the path to the dark side. Fear leads to anger. Anger leads to hate. Hate leads to suffering.'

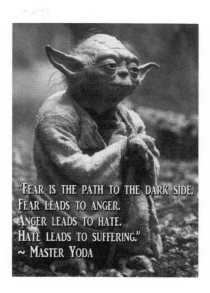

"FEAR IS THE PATH TO THE DARK SIDE. FEAR LEADS TO ANGER. ANGER LEADS TO HATE. HATE LEADS TO SUFFERING."
~ MASTER YODA

Armed only with more names and addresses and a slightly enhanced readiness for unexpected drama, we dashed back out into the local streets of Manchester for an evening session along the arctic, dimly-lit avenues. Dinner time was not the best as people are naturally perturbed when distracted from their evening fare, but we had some productive chats with a few easy-going Mancunians. I don't know if the folks from the Manchester in the Granite State share the same demonym for themselves as those from their more internationally recognisable counterpart in Lancashire, where Posh Spice's duck-voiced husband once scored plenty of fancy, curling goals from free kicks just outside the area (the goal square that is, not Lancashire, which would be impressive).

The night's chill was descending fast though and our contact rate was pretty low, so we took the advice of one creative sign next to the door of a prospective voter,

'Come in if you're Tom Brady. Otherwise, piss off,' or words to that effect.

This, rather directly, reconfirmed the fact that we were deep in Patriots heartland and their golden boy (before defecting to the Buccaneers, perhaps) was a deity regarded as being in rarified air almost approaching that of Jordan in Chicago in the 90s, or so I was told.

We were fairly quick to take this prescient advice, as neither of us were involved in 'Deflategate', and Frank needed to drive back down to meet some friends somewhere down near Long Island Sound that evening. The motivated lad was also heading out to California in the coming weeks to continue his newfound political spruiking (showy salesmanship) skills for Cenk Uygur in his challenge against the establishment candidate in his home district in LA.

He very kindly dropped me back at my hotel before continuing on his merry way and we wished each other the best as we parted. He's a quality lad and I will remember his fine company shared throughout an eventful day.

Although I wouldn't go quite as far as John Oliver's obsession with the offspring of Han and Leia,

> 'Step on my throat, Adam Driver, you rudely large man. Break my fingers, you brooding mountain. Shatter my knees, you fuckable redwood. Snap off my toes, you big, unwashed buffalo. Sneeze in my McFlurry, you pensive bison. Ravish my lungs, you relentless hillock. Chokeslam me to hell, you nasty shed. Jam your mandible claw down my throat, you irredeemable steer. Slap a restraining order on me, you forlorn block. Beg me to stop, you menacing obstacle. Pull my heart out through my ear, you meaty oak tree. Impale my brain, you unacceptable monstrosity.'

YouTube: John Oliver Adam Driver supercut

F. Mini-rant 6 – Anti-War (Repugnant Republicans)

It was the coverage of the Iraq War that was the real eye-opener for me, providing the impetus for my personal paradigm shift when evaluating media sources. Everyone was cheerleading for it; not just Fox News, but MSNBC along with CBS, ABC, and media institutions that I previously held in high regard, such as CNN, BBC, the New York Times, and The Washington Post, as well as domestic and international affiliates filtering all the way down through almost all regional networks, newspapers, and radio stations. This was all at the same time that enormous anti-war rallies were being held in every major city around the world, and yet the mainstream press were very nearly in unison supporting, justifying, and when rarely required to, defending the decision to march into a foreign land that clearly had nothing to do with 9/11 nor possessing any proof of WMDs. They were aiding and abetting war crimes, in my not particularly humble opinion. Disgraceful.

One extremely rare exception in the US was the Knight-Ridder newspaper group, based out of San Jose, California. They had the audacity to consistently report concerns about the looming war, against overwhelming tides of mainstream pressure to fall into line.

'In run-up to the 2003 invasion of Iraq, Knight Ridder DC Bureau reporters Jonathan Landay and Warren Strobel (both now

working for Reuters) wrote a series of articles critical of purported intelligence suggesting links between Saddam Hussein, the obtainment of weapons of mass destruction, and Al-Qaeda, citing anonymous sources.

> *Landay and Strobel's stories ran in counter to reports by The New York Times, The Washington Post and other national publications, resulting in some newspapers within Knight-Ridder chain refusing to run the two reporter's stories. After the war and the discrediting of many initial news reports, Strobel and Landay received the Raymond Clapper Memorial award from the Senate Press Gallery on February 5, 2004 for their coverage.[5]*
>
> *The Huffington Post headlined the two as "the reporting team that got Iraq right".[6] The Columbia Journalism Review described the reporting as "unequaled by the Bigfoots working at higher-visibility outlets such as the New York Times, the Washington Post, the Wall Street Journal and the Los Angeles Times".[7]*
>
> *Later after the war, their work was featured in Bill Moyers' PBS documentary "Buying The War"[8] and was dramatized in the 2017 film Shock and Awe.' (Wikipedia)*

This was an outstanding example of an independent regional newspaper group being able to do real reporting and stand tall against the weight of pressure to conform to the requirements of media conglomerates. This was becoming much less common in the US after the passing of the Telecommunications Act under the Presidency of Slick Willy Clinton in 1996, pretty much gutting media cross-ownership restrictions and resulting now in 4 media behemoths owning over 90% of all media across the entire span of the US media spectrum. Sure enough, Knight-Ridder was bought out by a gigantic media corporation in 2006, rendering it unlikely to stand up to the demands of the US empire-building military-media complex ever again.

The powerful vested interests had their minds made up about going into Iraq and weren't gonna let any problematic things like logic, decency, or preventing the unwarranted deaths of millions to stop them from getting their grubby, criminal hands on more wealth that they didn't deserve.

The backlash against anyone standing in their way was also shown in the treatment of Joseph Wilson for penning an article stating that no yellowcake uranium was coming out of Niger (where he went to investigate having been the former General Services Officer there) into Iraq, as was being asserted by Bush, Rumsfeld, Cheney, and their co-criminals. For his 'disservice to US interests', foolishly putting humanity first,

> *'Robert Novak, in his syndicated Washington Post column, disclosed that Wilson's wife, Valerie Plame, worked for the CIA as an agency operative in an article entitled "Mission to Niger."[16]*

> *In July 2005, Bush and Vice President Dick Cheney's respective chief political advisers, Karl Rove and Lewis "Scooter" Libby, came under fire for revealing the identity of covert*

*Central Intelligence Agency (CIA) agent Valerie Plame to re-
porters in the CIA leak scandal.[162] Plame's husband, Joseph C.
Wilson, had challenged Bush's assertion that Hussein had sought
to obtain uranium from Africa, and a special prosecutor was
tasked with determining whether administration officials had
leaked Plame's identity in retribution against Wilson.[163] Libby
resigned on October 28, hours after his indictment by a grand
jury on multiple counts of perjury, false statements, and obstruc-
tion in this case. In March 2007, Libby was convicted on four
counts, and Cheney pressed Bush to pardon Libby. Rather than
pardoning Libby or allowing him to go to jail, Bush commuted
Libby's sentence, creating a split with Cheney, who accused Bush
of leaving "a soldier on the battlefield."[162] (Wikipedia)*

*This is all detailed in Joe Wilson's 2004 book, 'The Politics of Truth:
Inside the Lies that Led to War and Betrayed My Wife's CIA Identity:
A Diplomat's Memoir' as well as Valerie Wilson's 'Fair Game'. These
books were adapted into a very watchable movie with Naomi Watts
and Sean Penn called 'Fair Game' (not the D-grade action flick with
a Baldwin and a supermodel, which you'd have to imagine to be utterly unwatchable).*

*Also embroiled in this shameful govt./media collusion was Judith
Miller, writing for the NYT, who was parroting unsubstantiated,
erroneous leaks from unnamed sources within the administration,
claiming that Iraq had,*

> *'stepped up its quest for nuclear weapons and [had] embarked
> on a worldwide hunt for materials to make an atomic bomb.'*

*Government-sanctioned lies. Unchallengingly repeated and as-
serted by the NYT. These fictionalisations were then widely quoted
and referred to by Bush, Cheney and their evil minions, scurrilously
echoing these untruths back to the public as,*

'Even the New York Times states this to be true.'

This was a perverse display of self-serving circular reasoning, a logical fallacy designed to justify and empower the US empire's blood-soaked greed. Cheney, Rumsfeld, Scooter Libby, Karl Rove and other hideous embodiments of human trash were the main movers and shakers behind this now exposed 'Project for a New American Century', with Bill Kristol and John Bolton also up to their necks in this megalomaniacal blueprint, along with Paul Wolfowitz, Jeb Bush and assorted other miscreants.

In an interview with Amy Goodman (another one of my true media heroes) on her outstanding 'Democracy Now!' YouTube and radio show on March 2, 2007, U.S. General Wesley Clark (Ret.) said the quiet part out loud, by explaining that the Bush Administration planned to take out 7 countries in 5 years, when he spoke of a classified memo that a Joint Staff General revealed to him after a Pentagon briefing,

'Are we still going to war in Iraq? Oh, it's worse than that. He just reached over on this his desk and picked up a piece of

paper, he said I just got this down from upstairs meeting the Secretary of Defense's office today and he said this is a memo that describes how we're gonna take out 7 countries in 5 years starting with Iraq and then Syria, Lebanon, Libya, Somalia, Sudan and finishing off Iran'

Don't forget that George W. Bush was the front man and spokesperson at the heart of these criminal exploits. Don't let time allow you to forget that, nor the inexcusable attempts to ingratiate Bush into favourable elite society with shameful, revisionist tropes attempting to reintegrate his public image towards,

'He's just an affable old man painting pictures down on his ranch and occasionally offering candy to Michelle Obama as an example of their budding little friendship.'

Tell this to the people of Iraq and the families of the killed, and to the US soldiers suffering from PTSD returning to a country that gives them scant support, resulting in some being left to continue to fight, this time for their own survival, bereft of government support, on the streets.

I saw a movie the other day about the struggles in Northern Ireland at the start of the 70s; economically called '71'. In a moment of compassion towards the other side, one of those closely connected to the combatants rather eloquently describes war, if you'll pardon my French, as,

'Posh cunts telling thick cunts to kill poor cunts.'

Blunt, but perhaps eye-opening and enlightening to anyone who's been sold on the righteous valour of war in the name of religion, freedom and/or democracy. There's usually a little more to it, i.e. geopolitical and/or financial self-interest for those with the luxury of sending other people into harm's way for their own invulnerable benefit.

131

The people of Iraq have not forgotten. Convince me of a more deserving group of degenerates who should be hauled in front of The Hague to face the music for their crimes against humanity than George W. Bush and his gang of heinous henchmen.

'The struggle of man against power is the struggle of memory against forgetting', Milan Kundera.

3.

NHP minus 4: I am the Great Cornholio

I'd stayed up late the night before, huddled in my cosy room reading up on all the political manoeuvrings and goings-on. So I arose a little later than usual to see a blanket, more like a doona (thick quilt), of fresh, billowing snow gently enshrouding New Hampshire as far as the eye could see in all directions. I checked my phone to see the temperature, in Celsius, -17.

Oh, my lord. That's cold.

I remembered experiencing that exact same personal low-point in Korea. Once. It was about 15 years ago and I can still feel that day's stinging wind cutting right through my extensive layers of winter warmth.

I wandered down to catch the final stages of the breakfast onslaught; still long enough to hurriedly stuff my face with a wide assortment of now familiar offerings, but not even close to the previous morning's carnage.

Tom Steyer then appeared and sauntered through the foyer. He was surrounded by mingling minions and was quickly shuffled out into a waiting car. Bizarre. Surely he wasn't staying here, unless he had bought his own wing.

I felt good and smashed down a couple of coffees to brace myself for the trek out into the post-blizzard, polar fluffiness.

Another older lad turned up on cue in his dull-yellow cab and dispatched me back to my launching pad to more doorsteps.

I'd missed the morning rush and got a lift out into the fleecy streets for a solo mission.

Gloves off was lunacy, but I spent the first 15-20 minutes with my right glove recurrently on and off for access to my phone, the source of my pavement-pounding political purpose. I adapted as best I could by having hand warmers strategically placed in my right-side jacket pocket for quick-draw electronic updates and alternating warmth. Still, the extremities of my right-hand were starting to harden up. As soon as I got back into the Bernie command centre, I cut off the upper-thumb part of my right glove to allow information connections whilst also boosting manual warmth for my next stint, not to mention the bonus cutting-edge fashion statement.

I was comfortable talking to people. It felt right. There was a warm contentment that, despite the bitter conditions, I was where I wanted to be. Time and opportunity allowed it and I would have felt that I was letting myself down if I hadn't followed my free will, loudly calling me to be there.

At the end of a productive session, I retired to the nearest Dunkin Donuts to contact base camp and await retrieval. There were 'Dunkins' everywhere in this part of the world and this one proved to be a warm and convenient meeting place for locals to hang out and catch up. I don't know if this was just a winter phenomenon, but it appeared to be serving the same purpose as a park rendezvous of yesteryear, only with consumer requirements. Naomi Klein in 'No Logo' talks of the corporate appropriation of public spaces; was this an example?

I was focused on wrapping my ungloved mitts around a tub of hot coffee as a priority far higher than making contact with my transport. While thawing out, I started reciprocating the amicable greeting that I received, which, again, seemed to be enhanced by news of my being an Aussie. There seemed a high likelihood that I was the first from Terra Australis to amble into this neighbourly retreat, at least since the tenure of this current crop of cheerful young doughnut dispensers.

It was an undemanding afternoon for them, so they could comfortably engage in conversations, sometimes even wandering out to the customer side of the counter to have a brief chat, while always making sure that the serving space remained well-attended.

There was a young lad who was friends with the youngest of the staff (from the school that she was still at), who sat with me and revealed his self-sacrificing dedication to half-baked, right-wing political and economic leanings. We had a wonderfully fruitful chat. Truly. This was of course sparked by the unhidden Bernie buttons and paraphernalia that adorned me.

I really liked him. He was bright and well-spoken, putting forward excellently misguided theories that would end up with him struggling through life if all of his approaches were adopted. We traded polite, smiling laughs as we enthusiastically tried to make the other come to the realisation that they were talking out of their arse.

As everyone knows, but very few are capable of putting into regular action, the only way to bring someone around to your point of view is to allow them to think that they figured it out for themselves. Cow-towing to the pride-crushing admission of being mistaken, by openly adopting the newly-appreciated viewpoint of one's adversary, is nigh on impossible in a single sitting. Well aware of this, I focused more on asking questions that I felt were pertinent and challenging in the hope he might take some differing perspective on board to perhaps embrace and hopefully endorse at a later date. It was a lively and stimulating discussion. Nice lad.

An older gent then popped in and the girls all gave him the most happy and heartfelt welcome. It was beautiful. This fellow's wife had passed away in recent years from natural causes, and I could sense his understated appreciation of this kind and hospitable reception. He was a straight talker, a bit rough around the edges; a veteran (confirmed by his well-worn hat bearing his former battalion details) and then a tradesman of many years. He was of the age that allowed him to get away with some casual old-man sexism that the girls either found flattering, or pretended to.

Nonetheless, it became apparent that it was less debonair, old-school charisma and charm that had won the girls over, but moreso their innate awareness that this fella had a craving for company. Bizarrely, Dunkin Donuts seemed to be the place to provide this sense of community - his refuge from an otherwise solitary life, perhaps.

There is a strong creed in Korea which translates as 'filial piety'; the Confucian belief that younger family members are responsible for taking care of their elders. The Dunkin girls were instinctively acting as surrogate grand-daughters spending cherished time with their lonely single 'grandpa'. What lovely people.

Once back at HQ, I had to get a bit of a hustle on. I'd signed up to be a volunteer at the Bernie Debate Watch Party at an indoor sports arena alongside the mighty Merrimack, just across from snowy Manchester's downtown. The debate itself was not at all far from there: at St. Anslem's College on the outskirts of town, but fleeting hopes of securing a gig at that were very quickly scuppered.

So I trooped off to Ultimate Sports Academy; a hollow warehouse, like an astro-turfed aircraft hanger, filled with sporting memorabilia and recreational opportunities. I didn't know it on approach, but I was about to engage in some lively tossing into multiple cornholes. It was an open-minded town.

I was early enough to meet up with the crack volunteer squad mostly made up of inner-circle field office faithful. They had iPads at the ready to gather the info of all attendees. There was another crew who'd pretty much already wrapped up their task of technical set-up (big screens rigged up and ready) and seat arrangement, and yet another well-drilled gang manning an impromptu, but well-stocked bar (well, a couple of long tables) with copious amounts of pizza and lashings of ale (and a few soft drinks to boot).

The most prestigious and onerous task of all fell on my shoulders; I was entrusted with a little clickable, metal counter thingy to keep a tab on numbers. The pressure of this responsibility was almost unbearable. Thankfully, I came to the job with valuable experience under my belt. I had been a 'numerical pedestrian data accumulator' (or some such title given to make that most menial of tasks feel imbued with an inflated sense of significance) for a couple of extremely undemanding afternoons in Darling Harbour in Sydney in the mid-90s. That was with my still-scrawny best mate, Bolly (aka Skeletor, Davros, COTY, Dave), who is doing some proof-reading of this for me, so if this little aside makes the cut, it has Captain Puniverse's blessing. We came through with flying colours then and I was ready to excel again.

But first, those cornholes weren't gonna toss themselves.

We'd established all our respective evening duties early enough to allow a solid 45 minutes or so of free time. We were in a sporting wonderland and another group was just wrapping up a session of rigorous cornholing! A tough act to follow, but I was swiftly drafted into a pair to tag team in and keep on tossin'.

The cornhole tossing session was very pleasurable, indeed. It was surprisingly high-quality, too - plenty of sacks softly cushioned close to the hole, lots of rim-shots, some kissing the cornhole and occasionally nudged in, quite a few jubilantly celebrated cornhole-in-ones, and we even got to share the ecstasy of one or two slam-dunk cornhole shots that barely touched the sides.

Great fun! I hoped this wouldn't be the last time I tossed my sack at a cornhole.

"I am **The Great Cornholio.**
I need TP for my Bunghole."

Those of you who also grew up with Beavis and Butthead will understand that I kept hearing Beavis' voice in my head,

'I am the Great Cornholio! I need TP for my bunghole!'

Doors were about to officially open and I set myself up as the first contact point as people meandered down the entry ramp. I bestowed basic directions, steering most towards the nearest available iPad to lodge their details, except for those with appropriate indication hanging around their neck who were guided to where the press area had been set up. I dispensed my brilliant binary advice all while casually keeping count. Pure genius!

There was a mild bottleneck on occasions as people waited for an iPad opening, so I basically just yapped away sharing well-requited hopes. I ushered Michael Moore through with hearty greetings, and my 'old mate', Nina Turner, also floated by with a small entourage, making her look like the queen of the progressives, which she absolutely is.

With genuine respect, the press contingent was B-list, as the glossiest faces were down the road at the main event. I preferred our lesser-known lot. They represented regional newspapers, magazines, and a cross-section of independent websites, YouTubers, and bloggers. People less constrained by editorial overview.

20 or 30 minutes into the debate, I gave in my final tally; if it was outside a margin of error of plus or minus 2, I'd be surprised – I wasn't there to fuck spiders! I then shuffled over to some loose seating at the back of the crowd with the rest of the recently-discharged support crew. A writer from the New Yorker enquired about asking a few questions, and the paid staffers I was with said they couldn't speak to media, as they were not part of the campaign's designated press contingent. I was just a regular punter popping by to help, though, and, despite sporting a campaign-accredited volunteer 'necklace', was pretty sure I was officially unrestrained,

'Can I answer some questions?', I asked both the lady with notepad and Dictaphone at the ready, while also glancing at the Bernie staff looking for a green light, and getting unanimous nods.

She asked pertinent and open-ended questions that allowed thoughtful and detailed answers. I received encouraging body language and sympathetic rejoinders as she listened intently. There were focused follow-up questions and she never interjected. She flipped her little notepad on a number of occasions as she jotted down my comments and I'd also accepted her request to record the interview. I was eager to represent the campaign and myself strongly, and present both in as good a light as possible, and I must say, I felt satisfied with the result. One of the main campaign team sitting in on the session firmly stated at the end,

'Off the record, 'What he said!'

I wasn't fishing for an ego boost, but I have to admit, it felt good to hear that and I proudly provided my basic personal details for a potential media mention.

I checked the online New Yorker periodically, bad pun intended, for the next few weeks, but found no trace of my chat.

One of my greatest lifelong mates, Cavs (aka Dish, Andy), had called me for my birthday a day or two earlier, but with some time difference confusion had dialled in at 4.54am New Hampshire time, so he rang again now for belated birthday wishes and dead-of-night call apologies,

'All good, mate. Didn't hear a thing. Was catching up on some much needed rest.'

I took his video chat to the viewing area up top at the back of the sports cavern and pointed out Michael Moore from above to him and his wife, Karie,

'Better add him to your selfie collection.'

'I'll see what I can do.'

I sent this through to them about an hour and a half later:

'We asked, you delivered!!,' came the prompt reply.

Like so many of the Bernie identities, Michael Moore had no polished public image that he needed to project and protect. He spoke to me like I was a guy that he'd been sharing a few quiet beers with in a local bar – completely down-to-earth.

He spotted my Aussie accent and mentioned that a game of cricket was set to kick off ('Kick off? What fucking game are we playing here', Richie Benaud aka Billy Birmingham, 1992) after the debate, and that I should join in. I'd heard this and was considering that very thing.

'Doesn't a game of cricket go for like a week, or something?'

'That's right. And at the end there's sometimes no result.'

'Fascinating!'

'Yeah, it really is.'

We spoke for a few more minutes about the complexities and absurdities of cricket, but it could easily have become hours given the chance. What a genuine, engaging guy and a really good active listener; something that I pride myself on and always pick up in others. I liked him.

In Iowa, I'd semi-deliberately crossed the camera path of Jordan Chariton, the upward-punching founder of the YouTube channel Status Coup. Here he was again. He was one of the very, very few reporters to give valuable coverage to the Standing Rock protests by indigenous communities against the Keystone Pipeline being built on tribal land in North Dakota.

These were the protests that Alexandria Ocasio-Cortez was drawn to, just before the Justice Democrats organisation (formed in the wake of Bernie's 2016 presidential bid) recruited her to oppose Joe Crowley in the Democratic primary for NY's 14th congressional district, leading to her rise as a progressive superstar. If you don't know much about AOC, you soon will. The Netflix docco, 'Knock Down the House' is a highly recommended place to start for some background info into her political beginnings.

At Standing Rock, Wesley Clark Jr., son of the general, also led Veterans for Peace in defending the local demonstrators from being removed from their ancestors' land by powerful corporate interests.

As the evening was winding down, I saw Jordan milling about, so sidled up to tell him that I really respected his work as a frontline crusader for progressive media, and asked if I could get a selfie as a mate of mine would love it. I was becoming a bit shameless, but sod it, I was passing on heartfelt appreciation to my photographic targets and then sharing the moments with others who would understand and enjoy.

Jayce, a mate I work with in Korea, was one of the latter,

'Niiiice,' he replied with an uncharacteristic 4 'i's of enthusiastic feedback.

I thought about staying around for a hit of cricket with a keen local group of Indian (subcontinental) heritage, and the suggestion of ABC – Always Be Canvassing – almost got me to 'pad up'. But the offer of a lift back to my hotel and a chance to actually watch the debate that was the theme of the night's gathering, but at this stage I could tell you very little about, saw me securely back at my dwelling for a 2+ hour YouTube debate catch-up session on my phone, while snuggled into the warmth of my room.

G. Mini-rant 6 – Anti-War 2 (Deplorable Democrats)

Go Zen with me for a second and, as impossible as it may seem, try to empty your mind of all the preconceptions built up over many years and look at a couple of other examples of US imperialism through no lens other than the fact that these things undeniably happened and continue to happen. Let me pose a couple of questions.

Why did the US and allied forces go into Libya very few years after the true nature and illegality of Iraq was revealed and reviled by any rational, informed being? When did it happen? Who was behind it? Why weren't more questions asked?

How about the drone program? How long has it been operating for? Does extra-judicial assassination fall into the acceptable realm of the Geneva convention? How is this allowed? Why does this not get the exposure and analysis that such a blatant breach of international law surely demands?

Maybe get some revelatory context by checking out something like 'The Lust for Libya: How a Nation was Torn Apart' on YouTube, which paints a pretty damning picture about Western greed being the basis of NATO nations urge to oust Gaddafi, not philanthropic displays of selective humanitarian concern as we are always told when justifying an invasion of resource-rich lands whose people are always suddenly in desperate need of an unhealthy dose of freedom.

Have a little read of Jeremy Scahill's thorough examination of the drone program in 'The Assassination Complex' to get some insight into just how wrong this is. If you don't have the time to absorb his insightful 256 pages then you could do a lot worse than to watch the documentary, uncryptically entitled 'Drone' to get a better picture of the level of atrocity and lawlessness this program unleashes.

Failing that, 'Last Week Tonight' yet again showed that comedians commonly provide greater illumination and acumen on such power-sensitive topics, which the limitless resources of corporate media giants consistently fail to bring to light.

YouTube: Drones: Last Week Tonight with John Oliver (HBO)

Just under 13 minutes of John Oliver will unveil revelations un-exposed by vast organisations, such as the Washington Post (owned by the horrendous human being, Jeff Bezos, now predicted to become the world's first trillionaire), whose motto is,

> *'Democracy dies in darkness'*

Maybe shine some light on this.

Bezos' Amazon has major financial ties with the CIA, having set up its cloud storage program for a lazy 600 million, amongst other top-level connections with organisations that it is supposed to hold publicly accountable. I wonder whether this has any effect on their trickle-down editorial decision making.

Do you think the Western media would allow, say, Putin or Xi Jinping, making a witty jest to the tables of media personalities, selectively inattentive to Western abominations (bombing nations?), supping at the well of power at another one of those correspondents' dinners, such as when Obama playfully gibed,

> *'(The) Jonas Brothers are here, they're out there somewhere. Sasha and Malia are huge fans, but boys, don't get any ideas. Two words for you: predator drones. You'll never see it coming'?*

Much guffawing from the snouts-in-the-trough, big name media identities at the japery of Obama's jest about stealth weaponry that routinely kills foreign nationals outside the theatre of war based on unaccountable intelligence, resulting in the 'unfortunate' collateral death of civilians, except when a double-tap strike is ordered and the resultant civilian mortalities are less accidental.

This is explained in extensive, sickening detail by Jeremy Scahill and others in displays of real investigative journalism about a topic which generally hides so high above the consciousness of most in the

Western world that this serves as a suitable metaphor for the remotely-operated hidden deathbots, which lurk menacingly unseen way above. Wikipedia, here, gives a brief insight,

> *'Ben Emmerson, special investigator for the United Nations Human Rights Council[1], said that U.S. drone strikes may have violated international humanitarian law.[13][14] The Intercept reported, "Between January 2012 and February 2013, U.S. special operations airstrikes [in northeastern Afghanistan] killed more than 200 people. Of those, only 35 were the intended targets. During one five-month period of the operation, according to the documents, nearly 90 percent of the people killed in airstrikes were not the intended targets."[15][16] In the United States drone strikes are used to lessen the number of casualties since there is no one that has to physically fight in combat. Being able to send drones to fight reduces the number of American lives lost substantially.[17] The U.S had increased the use of drone strikes significantly during Obama's presidency compared to Bush's.[18]With the help from joint defense facility at Pine Gap, which locates targets by intercepting radio signals, the U.S. is double-tap drone striking.'*

I'm sure the Western world and related media would be equally effusive in regaling such comedic references, as Obama's, to illegal barbarity if it were taking place in, let's say, Oxford, Sydney, Toronto, Auckland, or Denver (a city for each of the 5 Eyes) rather than places in Afghanistan, Pakistan, Syria, Iraq, Somalia, and Yemen. The US has been using the blanket term 'War on Terror' to universally justify unlawful killings on foreign soil. As Aussie comedian Steve Hughes puts it,

> *'[Of] the lies we're inflicted with in the 21st Century; the 'War on Terror' is the ultimate one. How can you have a war on terror? What are you talking about? This doesn't even make sense. When's this going to end? When they've got the terror?*
>
> *Relax, it's all gone. We're moving on to horror next.*
>
> *This is insanity. You can't have a war on terror.*
>
> *You're having a war on terror, are ya?*
>
> *That's right.*
>
> *What does war create?*
>
> *Ah… terror.*
>
> *Exactly. So you're having a war against the consequence of the actions you're involved in.*
>
> *But, ah, you know, ours is good terror. It's good, peace, freedom-loving terror. You know, kinda like terror-lite, sort of a diet terror, sort of a 'I can't believe it's not terror"*

YouTube: Steve Hughes on war on terror, global warming and X-factor.

Still Zen?

4.

NHP minus 3: Let's See what this Smarmy Jumped-Up Little Prick has to Say for Himself

Wandering down into the morning feast-zone, I was surrounded by a swarm of peppy, fresh-faced teenagers, who'd been bussed up from an exclusive NY prep school to canvass for Pete. I vividly remember the smug looks from these enthusiastically entitled 17-year-olds, when crammed into a lift (elevator) with a huddle of them, after they'd seen my Bernie affiliation. Their teacher was leading this pack and he and I had a brief exchange, dominated by his over-friendly disbelief about my mission. It came across as condescending, but I felt above it.

These 'rich kids for Pete' were not old enough to vote, but had been recruited to spread the 'High Hopes' dance routine for pretentious Pete.

YouTube: Pete Buttigieg High Hopes Dance

About to book another battered old cab unchanged in appearance or driver's worldview since well into the previous millennium, I remembered that I'd spent the last of my cash-on-hand the previous day. This hadn't concerned me as I knew there was an ATM conveniently located in my hotel just around the corner from reception.

'Unrecognised card error.'

Not a big problem. I'd find a friendlier money machine in town. Ah, but how will I get there other than tiptoeing along the now super shiny footpaths (sidewalks) and across the icy bridge?

I went over to the efficient lad at reception to enquire about perhaps putting 20 bucks on my bill and grabbing that in cash to get my day started.

'What about Uber?'

Ah, yes. Idiot. Get with the real world.

Now having the time and opportunity to sort this out, I realised how simple it was to set up and how much easier an Uber-ed up life on the road is. Should've been on this well before. Anyway, better late than never.

Sending out my first Uber request, I was excited to see all my potential pick-ups crawling around my phone screen like bugs in some Pacman-era computer game. Rather than waiting my standard 20 minutes for a lover of 70s rock to steer his sputtering, weather-beaten vehicle to me, it was a mere matter of minutes before my ride arrived.

As were almost all of my many Uber rides over the remainder of this US jaunt, the driver was younger, less WASPy, and driving a smaller, foreign car that was both colourful and shiny, i.e. Emil, a young father, driving a zippy little purple Honda. The conversations were clean and friendly, too. Political talk was gentle, smooth, and far more like-minded. I wasn't exactly sure of my opinion about what Uber had done to those traditionalists still driving last-century's cabs, whose welfare was undoubtedly affected, but my experiences were all Uber-positive.

Julie and Marc were friends who had made their way over from rural Oregon and LA, respectively, for the same reasons that had tractor-beamed me into Bernieland. Marc was old school (a little technophobic), after a lifetime of activism with pen and paper that he wasn't yet ready to give up on, but Julie was well up to speed on digital campaigning. A tech-savvy youngster was linked up with Marc to form a dream team duo of youth and experience. Julie and I pooled our more balanced resources by also teaming up to head out into the chill.

Not before grabbing a healthy supply of hand-warmers, though - those little packs of chemical magic which, simply snapped, unleash a square of unrelenting heat. I kept finding old ones the next day that still hadn't given up on their task.

Plastic ponchos were also donned as the snow had turned to sleet in the receding sub-arctic conditions.

Julie and I (seen here with our driver, Derek) were a good match. She was an inspiring and positive partner; we shared smiles and laughs as we endured the inclement conditions, which often made door-answerers instinctively kinder,

'Come in. Would you like a warm drink?'

In this situation, we wouldn't impose with heavy-handed electioneering. Just chatting with appreciation seemed enough - let the Bernie buttons send their own unspoken message. We felt sad and sometimes conflicted when taking our leave, as some older folks seemed eager to talk more than the day's plan would allow, and we'd always stay for a good few minutes after the thought of moving on first crossed our minds. Some people were just lonely.

After a solid slush around, Julie declared,

'I need to go back and change my feet.'

The state of her new and improved feet would get a few merry mentions over the next few days. We restocked warmth and energy at home base then soldiered on into the well-shaken Manchester snow globe to complete a productive afternoon session.

Revelling in my new Uber-ability, I zapped myself into town, as the late afternoon sun was threatening to disappear, to pick up my complimentary campaign ticket for the 61st Annual McIntyre-Shaheen 100 Club Dinner. I procured my pre-booked admittance at Shoppers, the 'Bernie bar' downtown, just across the road from the SNHU (Southern New Hampshire University) Arena, the scene of the evenings shenanigans.

Then I strolled over to the vast venue, where the Cheeto-in-chief himself was set to throw red meat to his starving hordes of incitable fools the night after next. Some of the harder-core Trumpers had turned up a couple of days early to practice their lunacy on the more rational. This was a true taste of the circus. Chaotic entertainment.

A few Donald devotees had gone to quite some effort to create a huge box of cereal with 'Corn Pops' emblazoned on it to parody Joe Biden's bizarre recounting of his childhood showdown with a local tough kid - the centrepoint of his rambling anecdote revolving around the fact that,

'Corn Pop was a bad dude.'

It almost seemed like Alice-in-Wonderland style creativity in this satire of Biden's trippy reminiscence of his wacky, youthful adventure.

At the other end of the sanity spectrum were environmental groups, but some of them even resorted to dressing up as polar

bears to garner more attention in the political marketplace that rendered the un-sensationalised into irrelevant bystanders.

This gathering of oddballs of all political persuasions, grav-itating to the limelight, summed up the US political scene for me - emotive presentations encompassing a broad range of sen-sibilities. All Dem party candidates were on deck to give a short speech, so media minions were swarming, too.

I was in the heart of the show. I couldn't stop smiling and laughing. If nothing else, Americans know how to attract atten-tion. It was as if not being seen was tantamount to failure. This brought eccentric attention-seekers out of the woodwork. And all of this was just a warm-up for the real commander-of-freaks, whose extravaganza of idiocy was coming soon.

Wandering in to escape the numbing conditions, I did a full circuit of the political palace before sliding into a seat in one of the dominant Bernie sections. All around the Southern New Hampshire University arena were stands set up by each campaign to sell their candidate and some swag.

The Yang Gang guy was putting on a good show, and the Bernie benches were busy, while the Biden boards were barren. I went and had a chat with team Tulsi and picked up some Gabbard peace buttons.

I dragged myself away from the exterior promotions and into the inner shell of the ample arena for the main event. It was already pretty full in the first of what ended up being a few sections required for the Bernie contingent, by far the largest and loudest slice of the colosseum's seating pie. As I scoped for a seat, I spotted 2 of the regular check-in desk ladies from the field office, and they motioned that they had a spare one next to them in a prime position. Perfect.

I settled in next to Amy, a librarian at Manchester City Library, and a delightful person. Chatting away, I was mindful of my language. I found this to be challenging when talking about things that I have strong views about and I slipped in an accidental cuss and apologised to her.

'Oh, don't be silly,' she said in the tone of 'I couldn't give a flying fuck'.

'I love Aussie Guy on YouTube. You must've seen his work?', she continued.

'Ah, yes. I have.'

This took the pressure off as Aussie Guy wasn't the most PC chap; his schtick was vernacular vulgarities. Why limit your linguistic options when trying to convey your thoughts and emotions to full effect? Language was there to be used, not shied away from, so I embraced the chance to use an open range of expressive options,

'Right, let's see what this smarmy jumped-up little prick has to say for himself,' as Mayor Pete scuttled into the spotlight.

This brilliant, well-groomed platitude generator really got under my skin - he was such a slick operator, but used it to undermine the progressive agenda with his identity-politics cloaked corporatism. As a schoolboy, he showed great admiration towards Bernie, which he detailed in a prize-winning essay. Now he used his well-honed, profits-over-people McKinsey presentation skills and golden-boy darling status with big money media-endorsements to keep throwing Bernie under the bus. His condescension towards Sanders, who had been at the coalface of progressive activism for longer than he had been alive, irked me. I knew I was not alone in being reviled by this smug, holier-than-thou, corporate-condoned upstart.

Mid-way through Mayo Pete's bland reeling-off of policy-free, faux-inspirational, political Hallmark Card catchphrases, he put his self-righteousness front and centre, by throwing thinly-veiled shade at the hero of his award-winning high-school essay (with a dig at Biden thrown in, too),

> 'We cannot risk dividing Americans further (by) saying that you must either be for a revolution or you must be for the status quo.'

We knew we were in the public eye and didn't want to give fuel to the media's pyromaniacal addiction to magnifying 'Bernie bro' behaviour. This media go-to, by the way, has been thoroughly debunked, as borne out by endless amounts of research which are left unmentioned next to cherrypicked anecdotes and selective tweets (with no framework, context, or exposition of comparable amounts of 'unworthy' behavior by other supporters). The cheapest and simplest way to play up a pre-determined narrative is by highlighting a few Vox Populi interviews and targeted social media contributions – I daresay you could 'prove' just about anything using this slanted method these days.

To describe this Bernie crowd as being predominantly angry, young, white men would be comical and offensive, as well as disempowering to the female Bernie lovers in attendance – over 50%. Not to mention those present from a wide range of diverse backgrounds - a far greater cross-section of America than was being shown by any other candidate's fans.

But this Buttigieg dude rubbed Bernie fans up the wrong way. We weren't having it.

Biden had sod all supporters on deck and zero energy amongst the few who looked like they'd been convinced to fill a seat for the night. The Sanders brigade was different. We had numbers, passion, and background knowledge. Boos started to bellow out. I let out a few timid cries of 'Wine Cave Pete' and a few others around me briefly joined in. However, another committed group of Berners were far more successful in getting their chant up and running,

'Wall Street Pete.'

It caught on like wildfire. After a few warm-ups, it was soon ringing out with the 2 to 3 Bernie sections all roaring in unison. I realised that the whole class might get a speaking to from The Fourth Estate headmasters (principals) in the morning, but damn it was cathartic. I was giving it all I had and was loving it.

It felt appropriate and necessary that Buttigieg be exposed for the corporate lackey that he was, at the same time that elite media masturbated on about how he is the future of the Democratic Party, which once represented the working class. Sickening.

Sure enough, though, the next day I got a message from a great old friend of mine, who is very successful and lives in LA, to pass on the media's semi-reproachful warning,

> 'Hopefully the booing of Pete last night is more panto-mime and does not translate to the animosity that kept Bernie's faithful away from the ballot box in 2016, IF he is not successful...'

I understood this reaction from people seeing second-hand reports through the lens of big news, but nonetheless, it was disappointing to see how pejorative the portrayal of Sanders supporters was.

Bernie's campaigns strengthen the Democratic party. The default position of a hell of a lot of his supporters is 'otherwise non-voter'. They are only brought into the process because they are inspired by Bernie offering them policies that offer tangible improvements in their life. Thus, Sanders increases the Democratic electorate for the Dem Presidential candidate, as the vast majority of these previously inactive voters stay involved and vote for the eventual nominee.

Also, if people intend to berate any Sanders supporter who decides to sit it out in November (remember that non-voter would likely have been their original stance had Bernie not run), are they also intending to berate the rest of the approximately 100 million non-voters who are similarly uninspired to get involved each time a presidential contest rolls around. At what point do you think it becomes the responsibility of the candidate and their platform to engage people to vote for them? They are already setting up the same false narrative that Bernie will be to blame if the Dem nominee fucks it up again. You reckon the Dems could occasionally show a hint of accountability for themselves?

Bernie was no stranger to such pejorative narratives. Should he resign himself into being controlled and play by their rules, or unmask the corrupt system and be branded a troublemaker and unruly influence, as the hypocritical and self-serving gatekeepers use calls for civility to protect their own interests?

In his 'Letter from a Birmingham Jail', MLK unveiled how the most damaging player in preventing moral advances in public life is the,

'moderate who is more devoted to "order" than to justice.'

Amy was next up (Klobuchar, not the librarian sitting next to me). She called for the overturning of Citizens' United to get big money out of politics, and reductions in drug prices by taking on Big Pharma. These were disingenuous little islands of substance, which were surrounded by a sea of Trump bashing and calls for unity. Mostly, though, it was a platform for her to unfurl her stand-up routine of lame, middle-aged mum jokes. She wasn't funny, but she was confident and capable. And whispers were that she was terrifyingly driven and ruthless in private.

Then Joe. You could sense his campaign manager, eyes closed, head in hands, swaying back and forth, chanting,

'He'll be fine. He'll be fine...'

There were no teleprompters. It was 10 minutes. The idea of a structured presentation leading to an overarching summary filled with intelligent, or at least intelligible, rhetoric was ambitious. Just not descending into a maniacal rant about something that happened in the 60s was the best that could be hoped for. Fingers crossed.

'What the fuck is this doddering old nitwit blathering on about?', everyone said to the person sitting next to them.

Absolute gibberish. Heads were turning in stunned amazement at the lack of cohesion of a presidential candidate asked to give a simple short speech. There was a dull, awkward murmur around the arena.

Showing human decency, there was communal sympathy as people stood and roared in support when Joe started ramping it up into a fiery crescendo,

'We must do it now. So stand up. Take it back. God bless you all. And may God protect our troops. Let's go do it now. Now! Now!'

Yes, now! What are we doing? Not sure.

Yangster was a stark contrast. So relatable. Really likeable. There was a lot of affable rapport between Berners and the Yang Gang. This was noticeable in the response from the Sanders faithful as the UBI king made his way to the stage. Hearty applause and cheers. Yang was naturally engaging, commanding the attention of the whole stadium. He identified problems, i.e. the loss of manufacturing jobs, that led to the despair that brought about Trump.

He correctly labelled Trump as the symptom of a diseased system. He pointed out that Hillary's stance that America was already great didn't speak to essential components of the Democratic electorate. He put forward a logical, reasoned argument for UBI with historical references and real-world examples. Truly impressive. He was also a far smoother comedian than Klobuchar. High marks for

the Yang man - he later transitioned from contender to CNN contributor, and it's good to still have his voice in the mix.

Tom Steyer, who I couldn't seem to avoid, then stepped up
and put forward personable, compelling arguments that railed
against his life work that had made him a billionaire and allowed
him to be here tonight.

Next came Warren. Liz was that girl in class that you always
got along with really well. There was a natural connection and
you felt that you would always be good friends, at the very least.
But then she started hanging out with the doofus quarterback
jackass, wearing make-up that didn't suit her, and taking cheerleading classes. When you tried to gently tell her that you didn't
think these changes suited her, she sneered at you and walked off
as though you never existed. Despite all that, you really wanna
still like her, 'cos you think she's still a sweet girl at heart.

In the upcoming debate in Las Vegas, however, Bernie would
be the only candidate to say that he would respect the winner
as being the one who garnered the most votes from the people,
even if no candidate reached the corresponding 50% of delegates

to bring to the convention floor. Biden, Klobuchar, Buttigieg, and Bloomberg all said that, in this scenario, the superdelegates should come into play and select the candidate.

Hang on. Isn't this a democracy? I didn't realise 'demos' meant superdelegates in Greek!

This would leave Bernie needing over 50%, in a field of thousands, unless he could get the support of the hand-picked, establishment-backing, corporate-minded superdelegates; meaning he would have a snowflake's chance in hell of getting the nomination.

Would Liz stand with him, considering their well-documented ideological similarities? Would she endorse him when it was clear that she was out of the running and that he was the last progressive remaining with a chance? Or would she come up with some cheap, campaign-scripted, demeaning sexist claptrap that she quickly backed away from, as it so patently had no legs, to draw a wedge between her supporters and Bernie to undermine the realistic chances of getting a candidate into the White House? Was she committed to: universal public healthcare, aggressively addressing climate change, strengthening trade unions, championing the people's positions on housing, social security, public pre-K and childcare, eliminating medical debt, and restructuring the systemic hindrances (created through corporate control) that prevented real change across the board on issues ranging from education to criminal justice reform? Whose side was Warren really on?

'Et tu, Liz?'

I need more time, otherwise I may say things that I will later come to regret. I felt a bit damaged on the inside from her recent efforts. While never naively hailing her as a progressive superstar, I had perhaps projected unrealistic hopes onto her, which had heightened my disappointment. I always try to keep up a brave face, but my heart still wept the tears of lost opportunity.

Saint Bernard then came out to a rapturous reception from those in the know. $15 minimum wage. Tuition-free public universities and colleges. Cancelling student debt. Medicare-for-all. Green New Deal. Policy-based solutions. Substance. Clarity. He is the real deal.

I'd forgotten that Deval Patrick was in the race. And, yet, here he was. Obama's mate. As Governor of the populous nearby state of Massachusetts, he'd managed to drum up a large turnout. No enthusiasm, though. Did they know where they were going when they got loaded onto buses from Boston? Maybe a congregation of old-aged pensioners who jumped, well, lifted their good leg a little, at the chance to go on a road trip. It was getting late, though. They seemed sleepy.

It was, however, an accomplished speech. He did a sterling job of pointing out problems. People are struggling.

'We hear them. We see them.'

Well done, Deval. Anything else? Any chance of a substantive policy or two to address the causes of this widespread pain and dissatisfaction? No? Maybe some thoughts and prayers might do the trick then.

By this stage, the big guns had all discharged their ammo, although the Biden howitzers were more like pop-guns which had jammed. The backlash for such a blatant misfiring didn't seem to eventuate, though. I wonder whether the media would have ignored such low-hanging fruit if Bernie had bumbled 10 minutes of non-stop nonsense to a crowded arena, or whether they would have tarnished him as a senile old has-been unfit to serve.

The crowd was now dwindling like Bloomberg's presidential aspirations after the hammering he'd copped at the previous night's debate.

Michael Bennet then seized his chance to spend 8 minutes liplessly confirming his irrelevance to a retreating audience. At least he did it in his perfect voice for narrating a hokey old tale of life on a ranch in the 1800s. That's all I was looking for.

Tulsi came out to round out the evenings proceedings. I like Tulsi. She gets bashed by liberal media almost exclusively based on her anti-interventionist stances. Meeting with foreign leaders deemed 'baddies' doesn't mean that you agree with them. Obama was hailed for saying he would meet with any world leader, Iranian or otherwise. The Clintons spent time at Putin's Black Sea palace. These were held aloft as towering examples of diplomacy, surely the preferable antidote to militarism. Yet Tulsi was blasted from pillar to post when she sat down with Syrian president Bashar al-Assad. The cosy relationship that Rumsfeld had with Saddam, before he was recategorised from oil ally to overthrowable, didn't seem to have been subjected to this same litmus test either.

If Tulsi had been anointed as favourable to neocon interests, she would have been eminently marketable; a young, diverse, surfing veteran who was well spoken, composed, and presentable. But she spoke out against US foreign imperialism. So she was an unacceptable, Assad toady menace.

I particularly respected her courage under fire. She knew that every interview she went into was a trap. All the standard trip-wires were put in place, every question framed as though she were a traitor, and yet she would always stay calm and come out with her head held high.

I'm not saying that she is the perfect candidate by any means. She had blemishes and some inconsistencies, but just imagine if the histories and voting records of all candidates were subjected to the same level of scrutiny and disdain, i.e. Crime Bill Biden. I would have taken her over almost all other contenders, though.

She was never gonna be given a fair hearing. The writing had been on the wall for Tulsi since 2015, when she bucked the system by arguing for more debates and was kicked out of her position as vice-chair of the DNC because of it. She then endorsed Bernie. They hadn't forgotten. They hated her. She knew that and, thus, had nothing to lose, so just went head on into the storm with a strength and resilience worthy of commendation. She had principles and guts.

Was it any surprise that she was last to speak? She came out after Bennet and Patrick who barely registered in the polling, whereas Tulsi was points ahead of them every time. There was a Gabbard contingent and plenty of Berners had stuck around along with a chunk of the Yang Gang and a smattering of Warrenistas. The rest were long gone.

Hats off to her. Keep up the good fight, Tulsi. Your voice is more important than most in challenging the rarely discussed American military juggernaut of foreign crimes and unimaginable amounts of financial mismanagement. Money squandered abroad is money unspent on those crying out for help on domestic soil. This was outlined by Dwight D. Eisenhower, a Republican, back in 1953,

> 'Every gun that is made, every warship launched, every rocket fired signifies, in the final sense, a theft from those who hunger and are not fed, those who are cold and are not clothed.'

He also warned of the dangers of the 'military-industrial complex', a phrase that he coined, in his 1961 farewell address,

> 'Yet, we must not fail to comprehend its grave implications. Our toil, resources, and livelihood are all involved. So is the very structure of our society.

In the councils of government, we must guard against the acquisition of unwarranted influence, whether sought or unsought, by the military-industrial complex. The potential for the disastrous rise of misplaced power exists and will persist. We must never let the weight of this combination endanger our liberties or democratic processes. We should take nothing for granted. Only an alert and knowledgeable citizenry can compel the proper meshing of the huge industrial and military machinery of defense with our peaceful methods and goals, so that security and liberty may prosper together.'

Tulsi was reviving his voice on these issues. I hope to see her again.

Finally making my way out of this political compression chamber, I opened the hatch and realised that arctic blast was more than just a slurpee flavour. Damn it was cold.

As I shuffled down Elm St, Manchester's main drag, my only nightmare was trying to secure a driver in the sudden Uber rush. I was with a familiar face in Bernie garb who I'd had a good chat with at the debate watch party the other night. He proudly revealed that it was he who kicked off the 'Wall St. Pete' chant. He was a cracking local lad with an abbreviated Italian-sounding name; Vince, Enzo, Sandro, Leo? He was looking pleased with himself, like a mate of mine from school who told me that the proudest moment of his life up to that point was when he'd started a chant for an Australian cricket superhero that was taken up and boomed out by a packed stadium,

'Lillee, Lillee...'

as the eponymous strapping, hairy-chested, chain-wearing Aussie working class hero thundered in off the long run to terrorise English batsmen, spurred on by the roaring chant begun by my mate.

Getting a chant off the ground is all about timing, messaging, and gusto. The young lad I was with had shown that he had a natural ability in all of these. I passed on my hearty congrats and waved him off to his nearby warm abode. Still unable to secure a ride for myself, I went into a trendy little pizza joint and grabbed a slice to warm myself and justify my entry. Not long after my belly was content, I Uber-ed up and was soon back in my snug hotel to bask in the glow of an entertaining evening out in polar Manchester.

H. Manufacturing Consent

If you haven't read Manufacturing Consent, put this down imme-diately, find it, and start reading. It's the key to unlocking an under-standing of the whole shebang. It elucidates how the information we are given, and not given, is filtered through a system with a foolproof design to ensure that corporate viewpoints are dominant and any at-tempts to challenge that are suppressed.

Let's take a little look at the 5 lenses of corporate media control, as outlined in MC, with an example of each one and how it relates to modern US media organisations. Here are the first 2.

1. Ownership
General Electric owned NBC, i.e. MSNBC, up until Comcast bought them out a few years ago. GE, as well as its obvious power companies, has massive investments in oil production and distribution, along with arms manufacturing. So is it any wonder that NBC was not at the forefront of revealing the existential threat of climate change, which has been widely known in the scientific community since at least the 80s? What about an in-depth study into the effects of American imperialism around the world? Maybe an analysis on the moral am-biguities (to be very kind) of the US drone program? Why not? Because

it was in direct conflict with the financial interests of their owners. NBC's Iraq war reporting was brought to you by an oil company that produces weapons. A good, reliable, balanced source, no doubt.

This is just 1 glaring example of how ownership affects content. With 4 mega conglomerates (AT&T, Comcast, Disney, and ViacomCBS) now owning over 90% of US media, the cross-ownership and joint connections are not only with fossil-fuel companies and arms manufacturers, but also with Wall St. banks, fracking companies, private prisons, medical insurance companies, charter schools, top-level real estate brokers, police weaponry contractors, big tech (Facebook, Google), factory farming powerhouses, the NRA, mega retailers (Walmart, Amazon) etc. These oaks of capitalism are entwined with deep-rooted mutual interests. Obviously, they will never challenge their own power structures.

The other obvious point is that these gigantic, multi-national media corporations are never going to be supportive of any politician that speaks out about raising corporate taxes and closing corporate tax loopholes. As a result, in order to protect its business prosperity and financial status, major news in America has a self-interested responsibility to favour corporate advantages over those of the people. Thus, it is inherently structured to reject, mock, and attack populist progressive politics.

In a quote commonly misattributed to Mahatma Gandhi, the plight of a movement against a dominant authority is given voice as,

> *'First they ignore you, then they laugh at you, then they fight you, then you win.'*

Sadly, we are still stuck in stage 3.

2. Advertising

TV media organisations are not paid by viewers, of course, they are paid by advertisers in accordance with ratings figures. This allows for the commanding role played by big-money advertisers in influencing the media industry.

A prime example is the pharmaceutical industry's flooding of the airwaves across all major US networks to push their latest pill. For those of you who haven't been to the US, imagine sitting through endless promotions for medications covering the full range of diseases and disorders real or imagined from high blood pressure to penile dysfunction, diabetes to uncontrollable old-age flatulence, and high cholesterol through to depression, psychosis, and/or substance abuse, most likely brought on by being subjected to such barrages of doom and gloom day and night. This fear-inducing marketing has succeeded in creating a nation of paranoid, pill-popping hypochondriacs desperately reliant on their daily dose of drugs to get them through the next onslaught of pharmaceutical propaganda. Would a change of diet and lifestyle work wonders for most? Maybe turning off the TV might be the healthiest option. Then perhaps go for a walk.

This destructive messaging works, though. The move to start actively pushing opioids on the desperate is a prime example of this. More people died in the US in 2019 from drug overdoses than all US casualties in Vietnam: over 50,000. These companies are the bane of the nation; the Sackler family that runs Purdue Pharma, for example, should be dealt with like the corporate criminals that they are. If old-school justice prevailed these pharma execs would be worthy of public floggings in the main squares of downtrodden towns all across the states as a warning to other business sociopaths.

The only redeeming feature of these ads is the high-comedy of hearing the machine-gun rapidity of the final few seconds of every ad where they are legally obliged to go over potential side-effects, i.e.,

> *'May cause bulbous testicular protrusions, anal leakage, random male mammary secretions, vocal distortions, spontaneous*

bleating, exuberant running in circles, and unforeseen social-ly-awkward erections etc.'

You've gotta concentrate, though, as that all comes out in mere seconds in a verbal blitz of potential unexpected ailments.

The overinflated role of flogging pills, usually to the unneedy, has played a critical role in propping up the dying TV industry (along with inflated ratings from the Trump circus). Without this gushing tap of advertising dollars, the world of big media would be severely struggling, or at least be in serious need of some OxyContin or fentanyl to help them dull the pain.

The profit-driven medical insurance industry, which also pumps huge money into TV advertising, would be significantly threatened under a universal, public-run healthcare system, too.

So, again, do you think the media world wants a Medicare-for-all public healthcare system where the government would have a say in regulating drug prices, massively eating into pharmaceutical and private health insurance profits? Don't think so!

Would this limit the endless stream of Big Pharma and Big Med (to, perhaps, coin a phrase) ads that currently sustain the financial viability of the corporate media model? You bet your arse it would!

Or, to prevent the pharma-profit spigot being shut off, would they be prepared to dedicate time and energy to create a narrative against Medicare-for-all and fight to suppress and destroy any candidate who promotes cheaper, universal healthcare while giving glowing coverage to all candidates intent on preserving or enhancing the current profit-based system (i.e. Buttigieg's comically deceptive 'Medicare For All... Who Want It)? Bingo!

This symbiotic relationship requires that Big Media work hand in hand with powerful pharmaceutical and medical profiteering companies to destroy any attempts to turn off their gushing ad-revenue geyser.

5.

NHP minus 2: High-Energy Irreverent Banter Roasting Corporate Media and Politics

Swinging into the office early, Marc was looking for both a partner and transport. I could help with the former, but not the latter. Sid was up from Boston for the day and offered us a seat in his fine chariot to battle on beating the Bernie drum. I had immense respect for those who were making good in the tough economic conditions out there, but were still willing to pitch in and lend a helping hand to lift up the opportunities for those without such benefits. He's an impressive guy; a good-natured husband and dad who'd taken the day off from business requirements and domestic obligations (with the kind blessing of his wife) to swing on up into the Granite State to put in a shift for a cause he believed in.

This engineer from Boston of Indian descent and an Aussie professor from Seoul of British heritage couldn't have been on a more synchronised wavelength. We shared mutual nods while sharing references from independent media idols such as Kyle Kulinski of Secular Talk, Mike Figueredo of The Humanist Report, and David Doel of The Rational National. Sid was sharp as a tack and highly politically informed. What a good lad!

He and Marc worked their magic together and I flew solo, but we were never far apart, canvassing opposite sides of the road, or adjoining apartment buildings, in an effective morning of team door-knocking.

I was loitering around back at the Bernie base post-morning session when a bearded chap caught my attention as he was wheeling a shopping trolley through the middle of the crowded room towards me. Realising that he hadn't taken a wrong turn in aisle 4, I introduced myself and offered assistance. This was Raymond – a campaign champion.

The supermarket cart was full of foodstuffs to replenish the weary troops. There was a plentiful bounty of nutritious goodies to boost energy and spirits for the afternoon push.

'Great work! Did the campaign arrange this?'

'No.'

'You're a generous man. Let me chip in.'

'It's all good. Next time.'

Chatting away, we became friends. I was ravenous, so honed in on the bowls of fruit that he had purchased - scooping healthy portions into a plastic cup and devouring them. Then Raymond offered to drop me off for an afternoon on the doors with Ted, a fella that I'd had a few chats with in passing over the previous few days.

Ted was a 72-year-old retired schoolteacher from NYC. When he told me this, I thought of the book 'Teacher Man', in which Frank McCourt conveys a sense of a life in charge of a NY high school through a narrative of insightful interconnected anecdotes. If you could learn how to excel in that environment, the rest of life would be easy in comparison.

Ted had a wealth of understated wisdom; worthy of true respect and admiration. He was ultra-politically informed with a lifetime of activist experience under his belt. He kept himself fit, strong, and healthy in both body and mind. I looked up to him.

With his straggly grey hair and abundance of experience, he looked just enough like Bernie to bring about the odd mischievous doorway exclamation,

> 'Hey, honey! Come and check this out. They've sent Bernie himself out to knock on our door. That's quality service.'

He also had that disarming NY matter-of-factness about him. He called it straight, no mincing of words, so you always knew what he was thinking. I loved that. It was all out there. Brilliant.

We wandered together and I asked him about his political past. He spoke of the progressive hopes crushed in the 60s when the Southern Strategy and pot crackdown 'War on Drugs' were enacted to give authorities the strategic ability to target African-Americans and students protesting for peace and justice.

Chatting with Ted was instructive. He suggested that despite the current high hopes, the powers that be wouldn't allow Bernie to get to the top job. I kinda had an inkling of this myself, but he verbalised it very smoothly. He'd seen it before and knew how it worked.

He explained how the paradigm shift brought about by Bernie's voice, however, was critical to providing impetus for a surging progressive seachange. A top and bottom movement, or inside-outside, he called it. I adored absorbing his years of relevant stories and the perceptive understanding that they revealed.

On our run we had an almost gated community that formed its own suburb. Like similar rich enclaves, it was given a suitably self-important name of high wankery: Strawberry Hills.

This ended up being the last section of our roundabout route. During a rare moment of quiet as we roamed the snowy streets, Ted sang out,

> 'Won't you take me down 'cos we're going to Strawberry Hills...'

With differing lyrical variations, this popped out on a few more occasions throughout the chilly afternoon from both of us.

After all the improvised musical build-up, it was a bit of a let-down when we got there. By crossing just one road, a different attitude became prevalent. Here I encountered my one and only Bloomberg voter in the wild. I wouldn't recommend it – he was a right arrogant prick. Ted also had a direct (see heated) encounter in the driveway of one self-righteous fella who gave Ted his marching orders on approach. Ted wasn't the type to back down and slink away.

He held his ground politely, but pretty firmly. I was at the end of the same cul-de-sac, but was well within earshot of the entertaining exchange. So I stopped to take in the show. Soon after this lively encounter, he gave me a half-hearted apology as he admitted knowing that that kind of interaction does no good. No need. It was so honest, it just felt like the right thing for him to do. To have acted differently would have been un-Tedlike, which would have been disappointing.

He also shared a decent little anecdote of walking through the Strawberry Fields part of Central Park many years back. He told me that he was going through a rough break-up at the time and was wandering morosely, lost in thought, when he saw a lone figure ambling towards him. It was John Lennon himself, no doubt heading to or from the Dakota Apartments which adjoined this section of CP, which was where he lived... and died.

Ted said that he himself paused and gave an exaggerated 90-degree bow - which he illustrated for me - and that JL responded with the exact same gesture. He said they then continued on their way, without a word.

While waiting for Raymond to come and retrieve us, I was dying for a piss. Reluctant to ask a Biden or Buttigieg fan if I could use their facilities, I realised we were standing next to a fresh pile of driven snow. In the manner of one not quite as pure, I decided to yellow it. It was high enough to obscure me from affluent onlookers as I emptied my bladder. Ever since seeing a childhood movie (The Year my Voice Broke), where a character tries to see how many times he could write his name in pee, I'd capitalised on the rare opportunities to leave my liquid signature when outdoor peeing. I didn't write my own name on this occasion, but rather left a deep Bernie insignia, probably never to be seen by anyone other than the perpetrator. I did it half for my own twisted amusement and half as a little farewell to the highbrow Strawberry Hill-dwellers.

I told Ted. He loved it.

Raymond whisked us away before any of the Strawberry brigade discovered my parting gift and came after me ranting (fairly justifiable) abuse.

The Bernie HQ was booming. The evening's plan for myself, and it seemed many others as indicated by the swarming numbers on deck, was to get down to Derry, which was about 20kms (13 miles) down the road, for a live viewing of the podcasters, Chapo Trap House. My good mate, Mike, who I work with, got me on to this lot a while back.

Their relevance rose during the lead-up to the 2016 election after a popular group of leftist Twitter 'celebrities' discovered an online rapport so strong that they met up offline and started putting together a weekly recording. The Chapo gang now comprises Will Menaker, Matt Christman, Felix Biederman, Amber A'Lee Frost, and Virgil Texas. They provide high-energy irreverent banter roasting corporate media and politics across the spectrum, sparing only a select few who eschew big money and put the people first. They pluck some occasional low-hanging corruption and billionaire-agenda fruit from the evil tree of the reactionary right. However, their true wit and insight comes farther to the fore when reaching up into the higher branches of the 'liberal' left which pretends to provide protection from the heat of society, but in reality offers very thin shade. These harder-to-reach pickings are gathered up and exposed. They choose not to conform to the 'required' politeness, which Will described as,

> 'the utterly humourless and bloodless path that leads many people with liberal or leftist proclivities into the trap of living in constant fear of offending some group that you're not a part of, up to and including the ruling class.'

Amber coined the term 'dirtbag left', which they embrace in their highly-informed, funny-as-fuck dismantling of the systems of corporate control.

It took me a while to figure out whether they were comedians who talk politics, or expert political analysts who were funny. I realised, of course, that the simple answer to this conundrum was simply, 'Yes.'

Having read their book, 'Chapo's Guide to Revolution', and as I continue to garner more and more pearls of political wisdom from them, I recognise them as some seriously insightful political voices, who are also as sharp and satirical as the best. Respect.

Confident that I could arrange a ride at short notice, I asked around and snapped up an offer. Soon I was cruising Derry-wards with a carload of students who'd formed a pre-primary posse to hammer home some canvassing then settle in for some live Chapo. They were good friends and their iconoclastic joking around showed knowledge, insight, and wit that exceeded their undergraduate age. I was impressed. I know I'm starting to sound like a broken record when blowing sunshine up the arse of every fellow Bernie fan I describe, but bias be buggered; it was how I felt. They all deserved the praising rays.

Down in Derry, the room was alive. Approving roars greeted the evening's entertainers. Their voices quickly revealed that they'd been going hard on the campaign trail both by day and night. They were in sterling form; such natural affinity and rapport. To get a feel for the vibe of the Sanders movement at this snapshot in time, you could do a lot worse than to check out this podcast:

https://soundcloud.com/chapo-trap-house/392-live-from-new-hampshire-full-rat-mode-21020

The then Mayor of South Bend, Indiana (rife with accusations of injustice in their police department since well before these issues gained a long-overdue international spotlight) was copping both barrels. I would challenge any decent-minded individual who had been scrutinising the primary to have any sympathy for him (unless your opinions were formed from cable TV news). What a self-interested, corporate-crony, upstart little turd!

They gave a comprehensive breakdown of the nefarious nature of the recent caucus, along with amusing anecdotes about interactions with candidates and voters alike in the Hawkeye state. Matt then detailed the incongruously rapid ascent of Pete to be a national contender, and posed how the influence of certain high-level connections may have accelerated his rise. At the end of a well-researched series of expositions outlining the Buttigieg fast track to prominence, he suggested that we put such talk on the backburner and focus on policy issues - I was mightily impressed. He suggested that should present impediment enough to slow his progress. Avoid overreach, he preached. Don't hand out any excuse to be branded conspiratorial.

Intense, but measured. Very astute and full of humour, insight, and poise - I loved it.

Will and Matt issued a call to arms for the next day, asking for volunteers to put in a shift in a remote area of NH that needed a surge of penultimate day door-knockers. The bigger towns were saturated. They needed people in the foothold of Durham, home of The University of New Hampshire, to spread the word to the surrounding rural regions. This branch office was also walking distance to Bernie's pre-primary mega-rally with AOC and The Strokes that night (this made it sound like AOC was guest vocalist! Is there anything she can't do?).

Mental note. See you tomorrow, boys.

Amber gave a rousing read of an email from a frequent listener who implored people to get out of their comfort zone to give everything they had in this watershed time for progressivism. It was empowering.

They wrapped it up with some motivational songs for change with singalong words up on the big screen. As they pointed out in advance, they were better talkers than singers! That mattered not, as the crowd howled along in shared uplifting cheer. What a great night out.

My transport team of uni lads had very graciously offered to spin me back the half hour drive up the road (in the opposite direction to where they would be heading), if need be, but I assured them I'd find another option or just Uber it. Within a minute or two of chatting with the NYU law student seated next to me, my problem was swiftly solved.

At the end of proceedings, I informed the guys, traded Facebook details, and again parted with hearty emotions for such a brief encounter.

Nick had pre-booked an Uber to get himself back to Manchester and onto a night bus down to NY. I'd been managing to survive cashless for a couple of days, as I couldn't find an ATM that liked my Korean bankcard, so I offered some alternative ways to chip in for half the fare. He pooh-poohed me and said that he was intending to fly solo anyway and was happy to have the company. The short drive flew by as we delighted in reliving highlights of the evening and trading further thoughts on related matters. If all of today's youth were as kind, aware, and motivated as those I continued to cross paths with on this trip then the future would be in safe hands.

After parting with fond well-wishes, I re-Ubered and skidded back over the bridge to my evening nest.

I. Manufacturing Consent 2

Edward S. Herman and Noam Chomsky outlined 5 main filters that information must pass through before the distorted, pro-corporate result is released for wider consumption. They refer to these as the 5 filters of editorial bias comporting to the propaganda model, which is designed to manufacture public consent. Here are filters 3, 4, and 5 with references to the modern-day US political and media climate.

3. Media Elites

When searching for 'expert' voices to tell us the 'dependable', 'trustworthy' viewpoints that we should take straight to the bank (probably co-owned by the network), a parade of establishment-friendly corporate identities is routinely lined up. Pick any topic of economic or military importance and check out who's providing the 'hard', 'reliable', 'consensus viewpoints' on it. It's hard to go past the obscene role played by former generals, now mostly lobbyists for the arms industry, all dressed up and rolled out in marching order to the drumbeat of war chants whenever it comes to discussing the relative merits of invading a land on the other side of the world. This happens even when there is no justifiable motivation other than resource-grabbing greed combined with a megalomaniacal quest for global geo-political dominance. On the rare occasion that voices are allowed on to talk of the resultant deaths, destabilisation, PTSD, and overall horrors of war, they are drowned out by far greater numbers of pro-war advocates, revered with gushing admiration for their clout and import, having all crushed weaker peoples before. Pricks.

The same kind of elite voices are brought forward to support, endorse, and sporadically defend a wide array of corporate interests. Charter school advocates speak on education, real estate moguls give their views on issues of housing, and medical insurance executives bestow their 'objective wisdom' on matters of healthcare. Could you imagine if schoolteachers at the coalface, people being priced out of decent housing, and citizens surrounded by illnesses left untreated due to extreme costs were given a voice on national airwaves in numbers proportional to these problems? (We're gonna need a bigger studio!) A different paradigm could be in danger of developing - one which actually promotes helping people in need, rather than heaping more profits onto the pile of those who aren't.

In Howard Zinn's exceptional 'The People's History of the United States' he writes with this stated intention of describing events from the viewpoint of the multitude adversely affected throughout US history, rather than from the standard perspective of the powerful few who profit off this suffering. Compulsory reading if I were teaching this.

The current climate crisis (the looming threat to human existence) is a good case in point. It took 30 years of major media almost exclusively ignoring or burying the issue, and then, once it couldn't be suppressed any more, oil industry-funded researchers ('scientists' is too kind) along with affiliated lobbyists and execs continued to cast doubt on an issue than has been beyond contention in the scientific community for decades. This was shameless and disgraceful dedication to wealth over the health of the planet, or at least the continued flourishing of human life on our now perhaps irreparably damaged earth. This knowledge was available and known in media circles for over a generation before any decent light was even shone on it.

What would the appropriate moral stance have been if the media followed ethics that promote the greater good for humanity over the interests of major corporations? Was this negligence acceptable? Personally, I agree with the character Marcellus Wallace in Pulp Fiction, when he says that it's,

> *'pretty fuckin' far from ok.'*

4. Flak

The propaganda model is well-equipped to deal with dissenting voices. The way that Tulsi Gabbard has been treated during this primary season is a pretty good example. How dare she talk of scaling back military operations and presence around the world. During the Iraq War, anyone with the temerity to stand up for the ethical protection of human lives, both US and Iraqi, not to mention the resultant destabilisation of the region, was branded an un-American, troop-betraying, flag-hating traitor.

Take a look at Sanders' prophetic anti-Iraq War speech to an empty floor in the House of Reps in 2003 (thank God for C-span).

YouTube: Flashback: Rep. Bernie Sanders Opposes Iraq War

You wonder why Bernie has always been an outsider and the powers-that-be do everything within their vast institutional capabilities to limited his influence. Could his baffling stance of putting human lives in front of vast war profiteering be a part of this? Traitorous.

Others standing against the dominant corporate narrative cop the same treatment – first left unheard, then mercilessly ridiculed, and brutally criticised if they make it that far up the flak-pipe. This includes morally-minded journalists (as we saw before) who cannot thrive in corporate media, as well as people-powered politicians, who are just now starting to gain a small foothold as more voters (usually internet-savvy ones) are seeing through these filters and/or have started feeling enough pain to be looking for different solutions. There's a long way to go, but some cracks are starting to appear in this opinion-forming stranglehold and little rays of light are beginning to shine through.

Here's a little list of the US Federal politicians, who I truly trust to uphold the needs of the majority over corporate influences:

Senate:
> *Bernie Sanders (of course)*
> *Jeff Merkley*
> *Ed Markey*
> *Patrick Leahy*

House of Reps:
> *Alexandria Ocasio-Cortez (NY-14)*
> *Rashida Tlaib (MI-13)*
> *Ilhan Omar (MN-05)*
> *Ayanna Pressley (MA-07)*
> *Pramila Jayapal (WA-07)*
> *Ro Khanna (CA-17)*
> *Raúl Grijalva (AZ-03)*
> *Jesús "Chuy" García (IL-04)*
> *Mark Pocan (WI-02)*

Peter Welch (VT-01)

Barbara Lee (CA-13)

Katie Porter (CA-45)

Jamie Raskin (MD-08)

Joe Neguse (CO-02)

Andy Levin (MI-09)

Ted Lieu (CA-33)

Jim McGovern (MA-02)

Bonnie Watson Coleman (NJ-12)

Peter Defazio (OR-04)

Judy Chu (CA-27)

It looks like this list is about to get bigger, too, as the progressive movement starts to flex its muscles.

5. Common enemy

The cold war served this role admirably for the best part of 40 years. Redbaiting still works even now, especially with the older set. The 'War on Terror' has been a masterfully ambiguous way to justify unsanctioned military action anywhere, anytime in the name of protection against the amorphous threat of terrorism.

The most brilliant recent strategy, as espoused by Matt Taibbi in his recent book 'Hate Inc', is the war against each other.

Divide and conquer.

The polarisation of the US into 2 warring factions endlessly slinging mud at each other and firing up their bases with talk of libtard snowflakes on the one side against racist, sexist, redneck gun-lovers on the other has people distracted into blaming each other for their woes. Meanwhile, Fox News and their equally dependent rivals, CNN, MSNBC etc, thrive on their mutual-animosity based ratings and keep their TV news networks afloat for a few more years. Most importantly, however, this diverts people from banding together to rally against the real threat to everyone's wellbeing: consolidated wealth at the very, very top of the pile which takes more and more out of the working and middle-classes coffers, as welfare programs are cut, often in the name of austerity.

We are fighting the wrong people – the media has us dutifully following their lead by punching left or right to distract us from attacking the real enemy of the people, and punching up.

All of this has been perfected and Trump has been a godsend for the news world on both left and right. What will they do without him? Hopefully we'll find out soon.

6.

NHP minus 1: Up Close and Personal with the Progressive Flagbearer

They'd told me when I'd first arrived at La Quinta that they were fully booked on the day before and the day of the primary, so I sadly had to check out. I made a point of farewelling a few familiar faces, especially the front desk fella who gave a side-arm, clenched fist of solidarity, like he was pulling down on an imaginary big-rig bullhorn (after checking he wasn't being watched), when he first spied my Bernie buttons. Just to reinforce any accusations of pro-Bernie-fan bias, this lad was the sharpest tool in this quite capable shed and should have been running the show.

I then readied myself to head off to a Bernie Breakfast to which I'd gleefully locked in my attendance the moment I found out about it. It was at Bernie's favourite local indoor sports arena again, which was nearby. I knew how to get there, but there was no walking path and even if there were it would be ready for a speed-skating race. An Uber was soon on its way.

I had all my gear (belongings, not drugs) with me, so getting into the event through the metal detector was more of an airport-like experience for me than most others. Actually, the bag checks were easier than emptying my jacket pockets, which by now contained a seemingly bottomless collection of Bernie buttons. The burly security dude smirked as I kept reaching in yet again when it seemed that surely the well must be dry.

'Any more?', he enquired with an amused grin.

'I think that might just about be it. Wait on... Ok, now I think we're good.'

It was lucky I didn't try to walk through before de-buttoning myself (sound more appropriate than un-buttoning) otherwise the metal detector may have gone haywire.

I asked a few of the campaign crew if there was anything I could do to help, but things seemed well in order. So I was free to mingle and roam. Grabbing a muffin, Danish, and a polystyrene cup of steaming coffee from one of the metallic self-serve mini-silos, I firmed in the realisation that this might be my best chance to get up close and personal with the progressive flag-bearer headlining the event. A selfie would be wonderful, but I'd be thrilled if I got a chance to shake the unstylish septuagenarian's bony hand.

So I decided to forsake a seat in favour of a position on the side where it seemed likely that he would pass on his way to the podium. A few others were milling about in this area, too, perhaps with the same intent, but it was mostly photographers gathered here awaiting his entrance. I'd set myself up at the front of this throng and started to believe that I was a good chance of making contact.

One of the warm-up speakers was Dr. Sophia Marjanovic, who'd dropped me back at my hotel from this same place just a few days before. She's a proud water protector from an indigenous tribe and wore tribal clothes and markings to reflect this. Her speech was powerful and moving.

There was a large man standing close to me wearing an immaculate and expensive-looking suit. He was almost reflectively white, other than his ruddy cheeks. The whole package made me wonder who he was and why he was here. He looked like he belonged in a boardroom, puffing on an oversized cigar, cackling with other caricatures of fatcats about their new scheme to beat down the prols.

He was announced as the next speaker and strode out to put forward a glittering speech (with no notes) embracing and emboldening all that is required for a movement led by youth and diversity to rise up against the incumbent power structures crippling opportunities for the many.

He resumed his position beside me afterwards.

'Great speech.'

'Thanks.'

Don't judge a book by its cover.

The 'many' I just mentioned are those referenced by Shelley in his political poem, 'The Masque of Anarchy',

'Rise, like lions after slumber

In unvanquishable number!

Shake your chains to earth like dew

Which in sleep had fallen on you:

Ye are many—they are few!'

Ben and Jerry, of ice-cream fame, gave a more light-hearted, but nonetheless passionate, cry for a progressive revolution. They were committed lifelong campaigners for left-wing progress and innovative frozen confectionery. The bathtub of ice cream they had donated to the field office a day or two beforehand had been warmly (ok, icily), appreciated. Gotta be careful on canvassing days, though, to strike a happy balance between activism and chocolate chip cookie dough, in the interests of staving off bloated ice-cream-belly lethargy.

Bernie would be coming soon. I checked that my right-hand was dry and ready, in the manner of someone readying themselves for an important job interview.

John Lennon's 'Power to the People' blared out of the speakers. Bernie had arrived. He entered the arena with a beaming smile and waved to the crowd with the hand that I was preparing to shake. He was then led away from me, around the back of the podium, to approach from the other side. My hand tingled with disappointment.

That was all good. I was just excited to be there, up close and ready to enjoy the show.

As Bernie was about to begin his speech, his absolutely delightful wife, Jane, strolled over to watch her husband in action from a vantage point right next to mine. I thought I'd better cash in with something to show for myself to help overcome my deflation at missing out on Bernie. I was well-rehearsed by now and gently asked for a selfie at an opportune moment. She obliged with her truly natural kindness that makes me feel warm every time I see her. I was elated to experience this first hand.

She was recording Bernie's speech on her phone. It felt like she was a proud wife keen to capture her husband's speech at a work function. This was true, but perhaps not quite as essential, as there were teams of film crews doing likewise with big, professional 'movie' cameras. She was always herself, unaffected by now being in the public limelight. You could sense her sweet and caring nature.

Leaning back and relaxing into Bernie's spiel, I got a tap on the shoulder,

> 'Wanna help out?', one of the campaign team softly spoke in my ear.

> 'Yeah.'

> 'At the end of these more intimate events, photographers and reporters always try to rush forward and get in Bernie's face for gotcha questions and super close-ups.'

> 'Ok.'

She explained that she was gonna set me up at the front of one of the aisles with an agenda of impeding the progress of on-rushing journalists at the end.

> 'Got it!'

We sashayed over to the back of the aisle and then, as we moved down past those who were seated, we needed to crouch down and do the commando shuffle, hunched down as if we were moving through long grass and didn't want to be spotted by the enemy. She then left me to perform my frontman role.

Despite having lived in East Asia for the best part of 2 decades, I hadn't managed to master the squat. Most men my age in Korea could pull off the casual chat-squat, eat-squat, and/or smoke-squat, and that's just what I've seen outside of latrines. Not I. As a result, the only position that would leave me low enough to not block others' view, but be ready to get into action the split-second that Bernie brought his speech to a close, was the sprinter-in-the-blocks position.

So I was now about 2 metres away from Bernie, directly facing him. I'd just done a military manoeuvre to get myself into such close range, and had now adopted a position like a coiled spring. Bernie glanced down to look straight at me with a look of cautious evaluation and for a minuscule mid-speech moment our eyes locked. I remember this exact instant, as I was trying to convey non-maniacal vibes, with the danger there being that you try too hard and stumble into what you were trying to avoid. I aimed for a soft, reassuring, non-threatening smile. This seemed enough for him not to back away or look to security. I also opened up my jacket a bit more to reveal my Bernie T-shirt in an attempt to add to my friendly vibes, without going full Mark David Chapman.

The speech ended and I dutifully stood and held firm as my purposeful loitering at the head of the passageway was being put to the test by the oncoming surge. I did a pretty good job of

slowing the rush with arms outstretched to the side at an effective, but not over-imposing, angle.

The tide, however, was strong enough to require me to take
baby steps forward to avoid faceplanting. Bernie had stayed put
for a bit to greet the small group of supporters that had been
seated behind him throughout his performance. I was now being
pushed slowly toward him. I was facing in his direction, blocking
with my back to the mob in my faux-accidental manner. It was
becoming less and less convincing. Whether I liked it or not (I
obviously did), I was on a path straight towards Bernie's old-man
shoulders, as he was now facing the other way taking a few selfies
and engaging in jovial salutations with fans. As I moved to within
a yard or so, though, he turned back and was staring me straight
in the face. Now, almost out of appropriate social etiquette, I outstretched my right hand for this sudden handshake opportunity.

At that exact moment, another security man-mountain came
in to protect Bernie from the surge, that I was at the tip of, and
my hand was knocked away. The intervening human-behemoth
then turned Bernie away from me as he started to corral him
through the crowd. I was pretty sure that I was about to be left
hanging. But Bernie had seen my gesture and had just begun
his effort to consummate the shake before being bundled away.
Just before dropping my arm down in resignation, though, I saw
that Bernie hadn't given up on me. It wouldn't have been rude
or even awkward to leave me unshaken, but that's not the guy
Bernie is. He lifted his right arm up, across, and back over his
left shoulder and then twisted and contorted himself in order
to extend his arm far enough to complete the shake. It wasn't
an awkward finger-grabber either, but a firm, full-palmed, shake

of 2 or 3 seconds. Other than the obvious unnatural positioning required to reach over an ogre, the shake dynamics were spot on; no wet fish-ing, over-squeezing, early quitting, lingering, or double-grabbing. Perfect.

'Thanks, Bernie,' I added to the pile of gratitude he was receiving.

'Ok,' he deadpanned back, again showing a humble self-deprecation when being lavished with praise.

It was about as short an exchange as you can get, but a personal moment that I will never forget.

This handshake summed him up - literally reaching out at his own inconvenience to prevent the discomfort of others.

He's an old man with a comfortable life, who could have put his cue in the rack and kicked back. But he innately rails against injustice, which is why he consistently goes the extra mile to stand up and fight for others less fortunate. The physical and mental effort he extended me would neither have been easy nor expected from most 78-year-olds.

Here's an ancient Greek proverb that symbolises who he is,

'A society grows great when old men plant trees in whose shade they know they shall never sit.'

Revelling in my post-shake glow, I grabbed another coffee and started chatting with Chris, a musician out from Idaho, who I'd seen around a bit - easy to spot with his long, bushy beard. We were both planning to head out to Durham for the day. Lots of un-knocked doors beckoned and Bernie's rally with The Strokes wasn't gonna be missed by either of us. It was easy to line up a lift, and Eva, a lovely lass from lower Mass., came to the party.

It was a drive through spectacular snow-covered forests and fields out to a quaint little shack that was the lifeblood of Bernie's operations in the university town and spacious surrounding communities. We were there a little before midday, and people were waiting for the Chapo guys, Will Menaker and Matt Christman, to rock in and say hi before relaunching for the afternoon's canvassing. The place was bursting at the seams with the vim and vigour of volunteers. As people supped from their clenched cups of warming coffee, inspiring stories of what motivated those present to get involved were shared on a speak-up-if-you-like basis. One fella gave a personal tale of how the opioid crisis had ravaged those near and dear to him. He had the room in tears.

I had a good chat with one of this hub's chief operators, Anlin; an upbeat guy with infectious enthusiasm. He was equal parts surprised and impressed to learn that a middle-aged Aussie dude had wandered in to lend a hand.

As I believe I mentioned before, I'd been reading the Chapo gang's book which was now in my bag in Eva's car. I should get them to sign it. Eva gave me her keys and I went to retrieve it. After negotiating my way past an irate teenager, tracking down drivers who'd failed to pay the exorbitant hourly rate in the oversized small-town shopping centre carpark, I returned with the book.

When Will and Matt from the Chapo team moseyed in, the room lit up with admiration, but I believe the heartfelt appreciation was moreso for the targeted fire that they had ignited for the campaign. They both gave humble short speeches to confirm that their focus was honed in on whatever was in the best interests for Bernie's chances.

One of them, I can't remember which, even deflected attention from himself to call on yours truly,

'I hear there's even some Aussie guy out here to pitch in.'

Anlin was their contact man and had shared the news of his new antipodean acquaintance.

'I just had to be here. I understand, like all of you, how important this is, and not only for the US,' I offered to the room.

As I asked them to put pen to their pages with a message to my mate Mike, who was more of a devotee than I and deserved a signed edition as thanks for steering me Chapowards, I added (almost word for word from memory),

'I knew you guys were funny bastards, but you're seriously smart motherfuckers, too.'

The shameless swearing was thrown in without offense - almost as an homage. If you've ever heard their work, you'd understand.

The campaign chiefs told us that numbers had swollen so much that all afternoon canvassing slots were now filled, but if people wanted to work as volunteer staff at the rally, they still needed more hands on deck. Chris and I traded a quick glance and mutual soft nod. Great.

Ted was out there, too, with a NY friend. The 4 of us navigated the icy path to the nearby shopping centre and were in swift agreement to frequent the oasis of nutrition found in a yuppie little health hut.

Savouring my much-needed chickpea and broccoli salad (or something similar), the Chapo boys, perhaps in an effort to balance out the unhidden habits of their evening lifestyle, followed us in not long afterwards. We shared brief jovial greetings in passing then focused back on our wholesome meal and discussion.

Ted and his mate wandered back to help out at the field office, as Chris and I set off to sign up at the stadium.

A lone chap was proudly brandishing his 'Veterans for Bernie' banner out the front of the arena. The show didn't start for hours and it was far from tropical out there. We offered to go and grab him a coffee, but he wouldn't hear of it. He was a hardy soul with an honourable heart.

Once inside, they were assigning different duties by show of hand; it was a bit like being back at school. Chris is a very sharp lad, and he was quick to suss out that the best option was to check for press credentials in the section that was front and centre facing the stage. Our arms shot up and we were selected for this ideal role. The evening was shaping up nicely.

2 quality fellas joined us in this detail - a strapping lad from NY and Mark from Connecticut, who was a beast, so we were in good company in case some of the press contingent got rowdy.

With an hour or two to kill, we chatted while watching the bands warm up and do sound tests etc. Sunflower Bean, the pre-rally band, struck all the right chords for me (sorry, that's bad) with a foxy female rocker blasting out the catchy lead lyrics with unbridled passion. We took turns wandering down to be the only non-roadie related viewers, standing in the best possible place to take it all in - right at the front of what would soon become a heaving mosh-pit.

We did the same when The Strokes went through their paces. Awesome. An exclusive front-row session for a band that was about to enliven an adoring arena. Happy days.

We also had a chance to wander around the Whittemore Center's (where we were) top perimeter and just get a feel for the place. It was where 'The Wildcats' (UNH teams) strutted their stuff, in particular their powerhouse (ice) hockey team, it seemed. Some of their famous old boys included such greats, if a silly name was the key marker, as Pepper Martin and 'Whoop' Snively. Wonder what Whoop's up to these days.

Speaking of silliness, this gumboot-headed freak, who called himself 'Vermin Supreme', was also doing the rounds lapping up the attention he so obviously craved. He was odd, but there was a hint that it was all a show. His mini-entourage of die-hard disciples, however, seemed truly bonkers. One goggle-eyed close-talker was babbling nonsense at me from about 7cms, convinced that she could convert me from this Bernie caper to join her as a fanatical Vermin groupie. So close. I think she may have almost started speaking in tongues at one stage. Amusing, but a little unsettling.

We'd been watching the ever-stretching line outside winding out of sight for hours before the drawbridge to the progressive castle was lowered. When the doors were unlatched, this human snake then hurtled its way through the opening, spreading itself out in the crowd-surfing zone that had been all ours just minutes beforehand. After the initial onrush slowed, the less committed attendees filtered through, not without some urgency to find themselves a good place to perch their butts for the show, but nothing in comparison to the Black Friday-like door-opening mania at the start. We had to turn eager punters away as they aimed for our prime position, which remained more or less empty until just before proceedings kicked off. We were guarding this section's reserved seats for print media, so they could cruise in for showtime.

Sunflower Bean kicked off the evening 'with a blast of elemental glam-rock excitement' (thanks Simon Vozick-Levinson of Rolling Stone). The youngsters down the front were going nuts.

Nina then harnessed this excitement in her first-up, high-gear transition into rally-mode. The crowd didn't seem like it had much room for further uplifting, but Nina succeeded in raising the roof.

An A-list of progressive heavyweights were lined up to enter the ring. Cynthia Nixon, the champion of LGBTQ+ rights and affordable housing in NY (amongst a comprehensive and appealing agenda of people-friendly policies) came out to keep up the momentum with the already animated crowd. She'd run a strong campaign for NY Governor in 2018 against the leather-faced emperor, Andrew Cuomo. Cynthia represents everything that the Democratic party professes to be dedicated to when they choose to put identity politics out there as the key evaluative requirements (when the candidate's policy platforms are approved by big donors). She ticked all the boxes, in terms of gender, LGBTQ+, and, having played Miranda in the mega-hit show, 'Sex and the City', high name-recognition. The essential box that was left unchecked was corporate endorsements.

This is where Cuomo, brother of CNN's try-hard comedian and wanna-be tough-guy Chris (Fredo), held massive advantages with his deep imperial connections. The NY Democratic Party under his regime had been exposed for flooding the state senate with Republican-leaning Dems to enact a right-wing agenda in one of the nation's bluest states.

Google/YouTube: IDC New York

The Dem establishment big guns all came out to crush Cynthia's soaring prospects; Schumer, Pelosi, the Clintons et al.

She valiantly soldiered on and showed tonight that as an actress, she didn't fall into the category of celebrities that get political by jumping on the mainstream bandwagon years after their help could've help promote a struggling fight for justice. After the hard work had been done by others to bring broad exposure to an important issue, only

213

then would most big names turn up to make cliched and self-serving speeches to cash in on the uncontroversial virtue signalling. Not Cynthia.

She had always fought for what she believed in, against powerful corporate narratives. I'd been in a few discussions, sometimes in hushed tones, between dudes arguing about which SATC character was their favourite. I'll spare you my previous conjecture, as my now-appreciative understanding of who Cynthia is, has her miles ahead of the rest in my eyes, whichever role she is playing.

Cornel then strutted out and did his thing. I could listen to him forever. A passionate, modern-day philosopher and poet.

Then a moment that I'd been excited about for days. AOC was about to appear. I wasn't the only one jumping out of my skin. My press-checking duties had been taken care of by then, so I was free to focus and embrace the moment. The Strokes were gonna fire things up later, but AOC is a political rockstar in her own right.

Alexandria Ocasio-Cortez represents everything that is good about the future. The same group of Cuomo-backing corporate cronies had lined up their big money support for Joe Crowley, the previous incumbent in the NY-14 congressional district. And yet she prevailed, toppling this 4th-ranked Dem committee member in line for a juicy elevation into an even cushier DNC role. I wonder whether the fact that he didn't live in the district he represented had played a role in his congressional demise. He'd been luxuriating in DC for years, rarely returned, so seemed detached from any real connection with his constituents. Whereas AOC pounded the streets for months on end in her famously worn-out shoes, talking to voters, and finding out about their concerns and desires.

I wanna give a quick shout-out here to Saikat Chakrabarti. He left his well-paid Silicon Valley life to join the Justice Democrats team, along with fellow heroes Alexandra Rojas, Corbin Trent, and so on. When AOC's bid to oust Crowley started to really gain steam, he stepped into the role of AOC's campaign manager. With a lot of assistance from like-minded allies, he used his exemplary IT nous to co-ordinate ramping things up to maximise her campaign's snowballing shot at success. The viral video ad put together by Naomi Burton and Nick Hayes (of Means of Production – a new media firm promoting working class interests) was brilliant, the canvassing and phonebanking teams were superstars, DSA were onboard and the energy was awesome. Cenk from TYT, Kyle of Secular Talk, Mike from The Humanist Report, along with The Jimmy Dore Show's lead man all gave her vital platforms to promote her outsider's bid to get a recent-bartender into Congress. Amazing.

This spectacular victory put forward both the model and the inspiration for future progressive campaigns. She showed how to put a crucial chink in the corporate armor.

She didn't quite have the crowd-rousing intensity of Nina and Cornel (who does?), but she is so well-spoken, genuine, and caring. The audience were hanging on her every word. We'll be seeing a lot more from her. It was an honour to watch her in action. She filled everyone present with true hope for real change.

Shortly after Bernie launched into his routine, we (Chris, myself, and the 2 sturdy youngsters) made a move down to our pre-arranged volunteer meeting zone for post-rally team photos with the stars. We stood waiting near the side of the stage, watching Bernie go through his paces to a crowd eating up his offerings.

Faiz Shakir, Bernie's campaign manager, was just a few metres from us. I'd well-and-truly lost all selfie shame by now, so slid over for a chat. Faiz didn't need to focus too much on Bernie's well-worked routine, but the amount of time he gave me spoke volumes about his character. I was intending to beat a polite re-treat post-selfie, but he started asking me questions. The Aussie thing came up. What had inspired me to make it this far? How was I finding it? What had I been up to? Would I like to pop over for dinner one day soon to meet his wife and kids? Well, not quite the last one, but what a magic first impression. He spent a good few minutes engaging in heartfelt enquiries about some interna-tional blow-in. I think it was me who disengaged as I didn't want to over-impose,

> 'It was a real pleasure to talk with you, Faiz. I wish you the absolute best for the rest of the campaign.'

He almost seemed disappointed that I was leaving the con-versation. Nah, not really. Anyway, what a good guy!

Bernie once again teed up the top musical billing by introducing The Strokes with his DJ-from-a-bygone-era charm. At about this time, the mini-army of volunteers were guided into the loading dock at the side for imminent photographic opportunities.

Nina, Cornel, and Cynthia were already mingling and sharing friendly chit-chat. Tim Robbins appeared, too. He was impossible to miss; a towering figure! God knows how he managed to wiggle all the way down that sewerage pipe!

Anyhoo, I wandered around, pleased as punch to be there. A little gap opened up and I tiptoed over to Cynthia,

'My wife would be stoked if I could get a quick shot with you.'

I hope that didn't downplay the joy that I was feeling for this opportunity, too. I think the beaming smile on my face had that covered, though.

As I had pointed out to me multiple times, after posting these photos on Facebook, my selfie skills were shocking. You'd think I should've been getting better with all this practice, but no, I was heading in the opposite direction. Apologies to my selfie targets.

I was prone to angle the camera from way too low, to maximise as much neck and chin in the photo as I could. Upon arriving in Australia, directly after this trip, my 12-year-old nephew, Will, delighted in his new nickname for me,

'G'day, triple-chin.'

He was revelling in it so much that it didn't take long before it was shortened, as in,

'What are you up to there, trip?'

Haha. Cheeky bugger!

Tim Robbins was looming, not far off, looking down from on high. It would be rude to get a celebrity snap with Miranda only to leave Andy Dufresne high and dry. He'd had a pretty rough go of it with the dead wife, wrongful imprisonment, and aforementioned squirming through all that sewerage gunk, so I hurried over to make sure he didn't miss out.

Like a Lilliputian to Gulliver, I craned my neck back and enquired - almost vertically - whether he'd mind sharing a snap with me. He answered in the affirmative with that familiar understated smile that made me comfortable, especially because he could have stepped on me and crushed me like a bug.

I had no other option but to have my camera pointing upwards. That's my excuse this time, anyway. He's huge.

AOC then burst onto the scene and the group of responsible adults fluttered around her with giddy, childish excitement. Chris may have squealed in delight through his thick facial hair. No, I fess up. It was me.

As we were arranged for a group photo, no-one needed to be reminded to smile as a broad, cheerful grin, that was so commonly a feature of AOC, also sat naturally on all of our faces – no need to say 'cheese' (or 'kimchi' when in Korea).

Bernie came out and for the second time today I was within reach. There was no chance for a second handshake, though. That would have just been greedy.

He gave a short, very well received speech thanking us for our efforts. Everyone bounced it back to him,

'Thank you, Bernie.'

'We love you, Bernie,' which always, rather sweetly, makes him blush.

As we got into possie (position) for the group shot, I realised I'd have been able to massage his bony shoulders, and would have, if asked. Both Chris and I were in the centre of the frame, and with some shameless enlargement, this would be the closest to a Bernie selfie that I would get. There's no doubt that I'd have snapped up this offer at any stage. Very happy.

This little alcove proved to be progressive heaven. I'm glad that I didn't drop off the earth there and then (there's plenty of work to be done), but if I had, I would have moved on with a broad smile on my face and a happy heart. Glorious.

We roamed back out onto the main floor and The Strokes had the crowd in a fervour. I snuck up to the side of the stage to check out the action up close. It was loud.

As I wandered around to scope the various vantages, I spotted the fella who would've given me a lift from Cedar Rapids to Des Moines a week prior, if his car hadn't been full,

'John from Boston!', I shouted to be heard over The Strokes.

He was sporting an array of Bernie buttons that covered almost every inch of his shirt, putting my, not inextensive, collection to shame.

'Greg from Australia!'

We embraced like old friends who hadn't seen each other in years. We each knew 3 things about the other: name, home location, and that we loved Bernie. The first 2 almost seemed incidental. It was a brief and warm relationship.

I wasn't much of a mosher, so I stepped back up to the unguarded press section where I allowed myself to take one of the plentiful empty seats. I started chatting with Marty, a music producer with connections to the recently re-formed band, which was belting out a show-stopping performance in front of us. He was also a wealth of lefty political passion, and he enlightened me that The Strokes shared his leanings. He recommended a couple of good reads: 'Confessions of an Economic Hitman' and 'Against Empire', which he emailed through to me (to avoid Facebook) as both a reminder and a connection. I haven't gotten round to them, yet, as my pile of political porn keeps doubling every time I blast through another title. I haven't forgotten, though.

I got a message that Eva had to leave, so could I meet her out the front to avoid having to track down my bags in Mass… (achusetts – the common colloquial abbreviation for the state to the south, which I was getting almost comfortable enough with to use myself)? We soft-shoe skated back to her car then she dropped me and my stuff back at the front of the venue on her way past. I thanked her and wished her a safe drive back down into Mass. (there you go, but still felt a little pretentious coming from an Aussie).

Re-entering the arena with pre-approved permission from the staff at the gate, I saw that chaos reigned supreme on the stage. I couldn't quite make out what was going on, but could see a mass (that's ok) of people up on the stage and it looked like there was a bit of argy-bargy going on. I was soon to be informed that the cops had turned the lights on and tried to shut down the show, so The Strokes wheeled out their semi-appropriate protest song, 'New York City Cops'. The police lived up to this negative depiction, or perhaps just had an acute sense of irony, by storming the stage. The throbbing mob of moshers banded together and surrounded Julian Casablancas and co. to let them continue musically deriding the cops to their faces.

This ring of protection allowed them to play on. The attempted show-spoilers were forced to back off as they were outnumbered and the sweaty hordes were fired up. A win for the people against the police!

I met up with Chris and Albert, who I'll introduce to you soon, at the designated time and place and we were laughing heartily at what we'd just seen. On the walk to the car, I even managed to pick myself up a much-sought-after Bernie beanie from some non-campaign-affiliated folks making a quick buck. I'd have preferred to have kicked some more money into the campaign coffers - full disclosure: I would always give money to a US citizen to buy stuff, and then humbly request it as a gift (to comply with strict campaign financing laws). So the more relevant reason for this purchase was the fact that all official campaign beanies had sold out months before. I did, however, also pick up a couple more shirts to add to the official shirt and poster that Chris had 'donated' to me earlier, as mementos of this momentous event.

We walked past Derek, who, despite being one of the regular field office drivers, was looking for his lift, and carried on to Albert's car. In the commotion of the crowded carpark, we were trying to figure out the best exit to head for. Chris wound down his window and in front of him was old gumboot-head himself, Vermin Supreme, peering in through the chilled night air. Oh, God, here we go. What heights of performative madness were we about to be subjected to? Chris hesitantly asked him for directions,

> 'Actually, the one straight ahead looks pretty congested and I heard that if you go that way there's a troublesome bottleneck to contend with in order to merge back onto the main drag. If I were you, I'd swing over to the exit on the right there; once you get out, I think you're pretty much good to go.'

And he was spot on.

As I was trying to compute this display of extreme clarity and helpfulness, Albert revealed,

'He's a local comedian. 'Vermin Supreme' is a drummed up publicity stunt, prominent during election seasons. He's actually a really smart, decent guy.'

Haha. America.

It was a solid 45-minute drive back to Manchester, maybe a little more with the post-event traffic. We were somewhere around halfway when Albert got a call,

'Right. Got it. Ok. We'll be there in 20 or 30 minutes.'

He pulled over and was looking to turn around before he said a word to us.

'What's going on?', either Chris or I posed inquisitively.

'Oh, Derek got confused and missed his ride. We'll go back and get him.'

'Ok, no worries,' we both added genuinely.

As Chris and I commented to each other later, Albert didn't utter a tiny sigh or even show the remotest hint of hesitation when learning that he'd have an extra hour added to his trip because of someone else's mistake. It was quite an eye-opening response; not particularly natural, but that was probably due to everyone else's expectations. We didn't mind either, but would have at least commented on the inconvenience, if Albert hadn't set the bar so high. As a result, the mood remained upbeat as we continued happily chatting away.

Derek issued an apology and a reasonable, yet not convincing, explanation, but again Albert's insouciant tone helped him to relax and join in the chat without having to dwell on causing any angst.

Albert dropped the others off at their respective abodes then ferried me back to his campaign safehouse. He was a quiet guy, but I was blown away by his level of natural kindness.

I'd arranged to stay with him a few days earlier. When I'd asked the field office crew for a recommended place to stay, a few voices chimed in unison,

'Talk to Albert.'

About a minute later I was on the phone to the most kind-hearted guy on the planet, and had a place to crash for my last few nights in New Hampshire. His place was like a half-way house for Bernie refugees looking for a friendly roof over their heads. There were others staying at this Bernie crash pad and there was a rotating arrangement of couches, floor, and a spare bed. My wife wasn't thrilled when I'd suggested that I might even try to pile into a local house with other volunteers. The idea of me sleeping on the floor of some guy I didn't really know with a stack of students in the year before my 50th birthday seemed stranger to her than it did to me, so I did what any self-respecting husband would do, and made no further mention of it.

J. More Media Musings

The corporate propaganda model is enacted through a number of expertly perfected media strategies, whereby there is no lying, or fake news, just approaches that suit the needs of the company's self-interest. The most obvious of these are agenda setting, omissions, and framing. Pretty basic stuff.

They get to decide what is covered (agenda setting), which, of course, also entails them choosing what not to cover (omissions). Then the general opinion of the network is made overtly clear, long gone are the days of letting the viewers decide for themselves (as made possible by Reagan's slashing of the Fair and Equal act in the 1980s).

All of these things mean that the media can exert a monumental influence over what we believe and shape our views to align with their corporate-endorsed worldview.

Fox News, of course, is the worst of all these, inciting anger, hatred etc and has become a media giant because of its appeal to negative emotions to fire up its viewership with daily doses of outrage and disgust.

The magically effective approach across many of the 'liberal' networks and newspapers has been to form a largely unified stance. Strength in numbers. When the Iraq War justification bullshit campaign was in full swing, one could almost question one's own sanity when seeing the relentless, across the board media consensus that war was the right course of action. Were the millions of people in the streets around the world all wrong, or were almost all major Western media organisations lying to us in self-interested, greed-based, shameless disregard of decency and humanity?

The people were clearly proven to be right. Meaning that pretty much every news agency that we are exposed to every day, was stupendously, self-servingly wrong. Don't forget that!

From all this newly enlivened skepticism of major media, rose up my desire to find better stuff. As I've heard her beautifully explain, Amy Goodman had the same idea, so she created her own news network in the aftermath of the start of the Iraq War: Democracy Now! This was one of my starting points. I have dedicated myself for years now to discover as many independent media sources and individuals who hold themselves accountable purely to an honest desire to portray events with a focus on a highly-researched, sober, balanced truth. Obviously everyone has their own subjective influences, but I have sought to find the voices of highly qualified and credentialled experts whose only agenda is to uphold the credibility of their academic reputation. I'd rather trust the word of a Ph. D. professor who is a lifelong expert in a chosen field, rather than get my input on the issue from a talking head of a media conglomerate giving approved views passed down the editorial pipeline.

I like to refer to such unfiltered expert sources as Academic Media; a bit wanky, but true. One good example of this is the user-funded online portal www.commondreams.com which gathers writing from such leading academic voices who divulge detailed analyses of current issues. Personally, I've found that by reading one (often reasonably long) article about a topic of interest allows me to glean a far more in-depth understanding than would be possible from endless 6-second soundbites or even mainstream-newsroom sanctioned press writings.

I do, however, watch and read a lot of legacy media information, too. I'm obsessed with seeing what news is presented and how, and

*comparing it to my own thorough research; my postgrad studies fo-
cused on this exact disconnect. As has probably become clear by now,
my main area of interest is progressive politics. Seeing the disparity in
coverage and treatment between 'approved' candidates and progressive politicians is to watch this machine in full swing. It is masterful,
and proves to be both fascinating and heartbreaking.*

*Everyone that I choose to spend time with, in Korea, Australia, or
wherever, comfortably has the analytical skills and the ethical decency
to come to much the same rational, moral appraisal of an item of news.
The key differences in overall opinion, however, are guided by what
news is constantly presented to them. My wife and I don't have kids
and I have a job that allows me more down time than most, so I have
the time as well as the desire to search deeply for my news. Knowing
many people who lead much busier lives than I, that option is less
achievable. Like any environmental influences, the news you get plays
a big role in the views you form.*

*I teach Global Issues at the university where I work. I've put to-
gether the course content and materials myself (updating them as time
passes) and have prepared a textbook for my students (Korean and
international exchange students). Here is the page just after the syl-
labus that provides some recommended sources for more information.
If you checked out one news item from each one of these, you might
just find some thorough insights into matters seen through the lens of
genuine experts who are not unduly influenced by the perspectives of
the powerful.*

*You can then compare and contrast these perspectives with the
opinion-shaping influences we are all continually subjected to from
those who own and run the world and have huge vested interests in us
all falling into line and not challenging the structure of the world as
presented by them.*

Topic	YouTube	Websites	Books
Globalisation	Democracy Now!	Common Dreams	Making Globalisation Work - Joseph Stiglitz
Income Inequality	The Hill Rising	Inequality.org	Requiem for the American Dream - Noam Chomsky
Human Rights/ Racial Injustice	Shaun King	Human Rights Watch	The New Jim Crow – Michelle Alexander
International Finance	Robert Reich – Inequality Media	In These Times	Saving Capitalism - Robert Reich
Shifts in Global Politics	The Young Turks	The Intercept	No is not Enough - Naomi Klein
Environmental Issues	The Ring of Fire	350.org	This Changes Everything - Naomi Klein
Global impact of food choices/ Water shortages	Secular Talk	Climate Central	The Sixth Extinction - Elizabeth Kolbert
War/Terrorism	Intercepted (podcast)	AntiWar.com	Rogue State - William Blum
Immigration/ Refugees	The Humanist Report	Amnesty International	Refuge: Rethinking Refugee Policy in a Changing World - Alexander Betts & Paul Collier

Topic	YouTube	Websites	Books
Technology/ Ethics	The Rational National	TechCrunch.com	The Assassination Complex - Jeremy Scahill
Women's Rights/ LGBTQ Rights	The Juice Media	CodePink.org	The Unfinished Revolution - Minky Worden
Corruption	Rebel HQ	The Nation	Dark Money - Jane Mayer
Education/ Internet privacy	The Real News Network	Truthdig Truthout	Permanent Record – Edward Snowden
Media Influence	Double Down News	Counterpunch	Manufacturing Consent - Edward S. Herman & Noam Chomsky Hate Inc. – Matt Taibbi

Movies:

Globalisation: The New Rulers of the World

Inequality for all, The Corporation, Wal-Mart: The High Cost of Low Price

13ᵗʰ, E-Team, Mandela: Long Walk to Freedom, Selma, Cry Freedom, Malcolm X, The Killing Fields

The Big Short, Saving Capitalism, Inside Job

Capitalism: A Love Story, Where to Invade Next

An Inconvenient Truth, Before the Flood, The 11th Hour, Who Killed the Electric Car, Gas Land, The Yes Men are Revolting

Forks over Knives, Food Inc., Food Choices

Breaking the Silence, No End in Sight, Fahrenheit 11/9, Syriana

Babel, Children of Men

Drone, The Fog of War, Why we Fight, National Bird, Good Kill, Eye in the Sky

Suffragette, Milk

Michael Clayton, Erin Brockovich, Fair Game, Goldstone, Enron: The Smartest Guys in the Room

CitizenFour, Snowden, The Wikileaks Documentary, Risk, Class Dismissed, Waiting for Superman

Manufacturing Consent, The Myth of the Liberal Media: The Propaganda Model of News, Good Night and Good Luck, Network, All the President's Men, The Internet's Own Boy, We are Legion, Propaganda, The War you Don't See, Starsuckers, Orwell Rolls in his Grave

7.

New Hampshire Primary Day: Slam-Jump Celebrating like a Pogo Stick on Speed

Bundling into Bernie HQ bright and early, I discovered with joy that Cornel was due to visit shortly to give thanks, love, and hope to us all on behalf of the campaign. Also to fire us up for an energetic final hit-out.

I've never seen him use notes, but he gave a speech of the most richly flowing prose that would take months for most to prepare. Off the cuff. It was relevant to the day at hand, spoke of the weeks leading up to it, and the future beyond, regardless of the outcome of contemporary elections. As always, it was infused with relevant historical reflections and hard-hitting quotes to perfectly sum up the moment. The man has some incredible rhetorical talent. He backs up his words with actions, too.

The room was on a roller-coaster ride of cheers, tears, endless nods and affirmations to verify the understood poignancy of this great man's message. There was a touching moment near the end when he spotted my canvassing comrade, Ted, who was standing near the back of the room. He broke off with,

'My brother, Ted. I didn't see you there before, my dear brother. This man has fought side by side with me down in the streets and halls of New York City for many a year. It is an honour to be here with you, Ted, my dear friend.'

Cornel resumed his compelling address, getting back on a roll with ease, and then, as soon as he'd wrapped up, proceeded straight over to Ted to reinforce his affectionate regards. They had known each other for a long time and this was easy to see in their familiar embrace and effortless chat.

Ted is a very understated New Yorker - old school. When I suggested that it must have been a powerful and moving moment for him, he downplayed it. After it sank in, though, he let on that he was truly touched.

Cornel hung around to give his time to everyone who wanted to say hi. A formal line was arranged and when my turn came up he also picked up on my Aussie accent and spoke with such kindness that my already blurry eyes did the opposite of drying up. I got moved on as we'd spoken for a minute or more and the line was still curling round the room. Not before getting my own short hug, though. It may have been a blink caught by my phone camera, wielded by campaign staff acting as photographic assistants, but I think my eyes closed themselves for a few seconds. I don't wanna bang on with any try-hard attempts at feelings of spirituality, but Cornel could bring out deep emotions from people -a childlike sense of paternal protection, guidance, or something. It felt right. I have a good relationship with my dad and wasn't craving a special fatherly moment, but it had a feeling higher than just a post-speech selfie. I adore Cornel West and was so honoured to meet him (more than once).

Like on Iowa caucus day, our canvassing app only flagged Bernie voters today. Ted and I teamed up again to venture out into the fertile fields of fans. It was another glorious day of congratulating, reminding, or pumping people up to make sure that every advocate for Bernie registered their support at the polls. To maximise our hit rate on this GOTV (Get Out The Vote) blitz, Ted and I split up to cover more ground. Most didn't need much encouragement - if you were voting for Sanders, you were doing so with gusto. As in Iowa, the air on voting day was filled with cheers, high-fives, and the occasional hug. Bernie energy was on a different scale to the rest from what I could see.

I was about to knock on one door at a house adorned with Bernie love - yard signs, window posters, and bumper stickers on the car, which pulled into the drive right as I approached. It was the parents of Bernie's campaign director in New Hampshire, Shannon Jackson, and they'd been sitting right behind me at the McIntyre-Shaheen 100 Club Dinner event a few days before,

'Hey! How are you?'

'Hi there. Yeah, wonderful, thanks.'

'I don't think I need to remind you to vote, do I?'

'You don't. We've just taken care of that.'

'Fantastic. Hope to see you at the victory party.'

'For sure. We'll be there. Keep up the great work.'

'Thanks. Will do.'

This was the sort of vibe that carried me around all day. With one exception.

I knocked on the side door next to the driveway at this one place, as a sign out front indicated I should. A scruffy-looking nerfherder bundled out and my wide cheerful grin started to waver as I saw he had a rather stern, almost surly, look on his face. I was guarded as he approached me and got within striking distance. Maybe he'd been daytime drinking, too.

'Hi. Are you planning to vote in the primary today?'

'I am.'

'Do you mind me asking who you're thinking of voting for?'

'I can see you're a Bernie guy.'

'That's right.'

'Why should I vote for him?'

'Well, I'd suggest because he's the only candidate that fully rejects any corporate funding, so I think he's the one that you can trust to represent the people rather than the big companies.'

'That is an excellent answer.'

'Thank you.'

'I agree and am definitely voting for Bernie. I just like to make sure that people understand why.'

Phew. He'd flipped the canvass upside down, and I went from thinking he might throw a punch at me to giving him a small man-hug, to register my relief. I got a quick snap with him, too, to mark the moment. He wanted to continue chatting, but I had to beg my leave to keep on hammering out more Bernie ballots.

We made our way back into the Bernie hutch, as polls closing time drew near. One of the paid staffers, Sus, was a young woman of Nepalese heritage. Her mum had prepared a vat of the most delightful curry to give us a primary day boost. It was so good.

Raymond, a young lad called Matthew, and I then set up an Uber to get us to the results watch (victory?) party. As we piled into our pick-up, a smiling young South Sudanese refugee who had moved his family to the US a few years beforehand greeted us with,

'Ah, I love Bernie!'

'Have you voted?', both Raymond and I blurted back.

'No time. I've been driving all day.'

With a sudden sense of urgency, as though a Bond villain's bomb had just started ticking,

'Do you know the nearest polling station to where you live?'

'Yeah, I think I do.'

'Ok, don't worry about the change of direction, we'll make sure you're well covered.'

'Are you sure?'

'100%. Hit it!'

We had 30 minutes, which sounded ample. Doors closed at 7pm sharp. He said it was about 15 mins away.

Peter is a cheerful man and a pillar of his community, involved in community organising for 'We Were Children (26,000 Lost Boys)', which promotes awareness and support for the children orphaned by the Sudanese civil war. He is also the very proud manager of SUPER STAR FC, where many fellow former refugees gather to show their footballing prowess. He had family in Sydney, too, and said one day he hoped to move down there. I was able to help answer many questions he had about Australia (and we still keep in touch through Facebook).

We pulled into his polling station. He wandered over with more than 10 minutes to spare, but soon came hustling back.

Wrong place. For his address, he had to go to the station on the other side of this district. No time to argue. We were off. The clock was ticking.

Checking for short cuts and driving with a sense of purpose, we closed in. There wasn't much time to play with. We waited at a red light for what seemed an eternity then sped off with everyone on the edge of their seat, breathlessly checking distance against time. Peter was a good driver and weaved his way as we hurried toward our target. I kid you not, we pulled up right in front of the voting location's front doors just as the clock ticked over to 6.59pm. Peter dashed out. We'd made it.

He came running back immediately, though, as the official out the front shouted at him,

'You can't park there, sir!'

We'd all jumped out at the same time as Peter, and with nervous energy abounding, shouted,

'Throw us your keys. We'll park it.'

He did.

'Ok, go, go, go!'

Success. He got in with, I would guess, around 30 seconds remaining. Deep sighs of relief came out of all of us. It was an exciting and empowering feeling and I think I'd have to try pretty hard to top that as the most active assistance I could give in helping someone register their vote in a foreign land.

He came out with a beaming grin.

'Thank you, gentlemen.'

'Not at all, Peter. It was our absolute pleasure.'

After proud photos were taken of us together out the front of the school where he pulled the lever for Bernie, he delivered us in a more leisurely fashion to the scene where we hoped Bernie would greet his fans with a victory speech later that night. We continued a buoyant chat with Peter, all shared our Facebook details with him then wished him all the very best as we joined the lengthy line outside the evening's venue, the Southern New Hampshire University Field House.

They had let the first large batch of supporters in, but said they were waiting for campaign officials to all be admitted next, before opening the doors to the rest. Made sense to make sure that the campaign team members didn't miss out. Polls had obviously closed and they should all have been on their way.

Results started trickling in and everyone was sharing news and reactions with others in the long line. It was close, but Bernie was out in front early doors. Things were looking good. Positive vibes filled the cold evening air.

News of Michael Bennet dropping out popped up in alerts.

'Bennet! No! WHYYYYYYYY?', Raymond and I revelled in dismissive mockery, with knees bent and arms outstretched above our heads.

We got in and mingled with many familiar faces. We slotted in to a standing position right up close to the podium next to Chris, who had gotten in during the first wave. There were still plenty of seats in the stands on the sides, but screw that, we wanted to be in the heart of celebrations, as close as possible to the victor himself.

The press was circling. I had a good chat with a lass from the Wall St. Times and gave her my email address. She contacted me a few days later looking for wacky tales from the campaign trail. I didn't have any great inclination to spend my time supplying her with anecdotes to be either discarded or used editorially, though.

Wandering around, I heard a broad Aussie accent from a female journalist asking questions of someone in the assembled group. Stopping within earshot of her discussion, I loitered ready to pounce and find out who she was. I'd positioned myself with my back to her, so found myself facing a young couple from an unnaturally close range.

'Ah, sorry to be a bit awkward, but I'm an Aussie and wanna find out who the Australian reporter behind me is.'

'Haha. All good. We've got you covered.'

Rather than going into espionage-style false conversing, we just had a brief normal chat until I excused myself when the window of opportunity behind me opened up,

'Yeah, go. Enjoy the night.'

'Cheers. You, too.'

I turned and introduced myself as a fellow Aussie,

'Sorry, I couldn't help but hear your accent. How are ya?', again dropping into my slightly put-on Aussie accent, as my former ocker twang has softened a little after years abroad.

'Yeah, good, mate. So you've come all the way over here just to volunteer for Bernie?'

'Yep, bang on.'

'Why?'

Yet again, I gave my proud little spiel that I was becoming increasingly comfortable with.

'Oh, yeah. Alright then.'

'Do you mind me asking who you work for?'

'No worries. The Daily Telegraph.'

This was Sydney's premier conservative rag; a right-wing tabloid propaganda machine for Rupert Murdoch's News Corp, of Fox News fame.

'Really? And, sorry, what's your name?'

'I'm Miranda Devine.'

'Ah, is that right?! Ha. Well, please be nice to me, Miranda. I'll be looking out to make sure you don't depict me as some kind of deluded Aussie abroad duped into falling for communist claptrap.'

'Oh, I wouldn't do that to you now, would I?'

I treated her question as rhetorical, as we both knew that she would. She even flashed a devilish smirk when she suggested that it would be beneath her. Nothing was. She was a bottom-dweller capable of scum-sucking, journalistic filth.

'Haha. Ok, well, thanks for the chat.'

I don't think she did out me as a red flag-waving Leninist, though, as far as my limited checking revealed.

Most people in Australia know who she is. It was only her face that wasn't familiar to me. Her amoral agenda preceded her. She had proven her depths of depravity time and again in a career of high-profile muckraking and sensationalist conservative mud-slinging. She is much less Miranda from 'Sex and the City', and much more Miranda from 'The Devil Wears Prada'.

Each time CNN was beamed onto the big screens in the room, projecting us into view right in front of ourselves, the scene would erupt in euphoric lefty love. Tallies were coming in. Bernie was holding onto a solid, but not yet conclusive lead. This was the atmosphere I'd been hoping for in Iowa.

A few of the regular podium professionals spoke with expectant positivity to the bubbling crowd. Everyone was either checking election alerts themselves or listening in as every update was readily shared. We didn't need to wait long to hear from the big man this time.

He'd led from the start and maintained the top position in every fresh tallying batch, until a ripple of joy very quickly became a tide of unanimous ecstasy,

'They've called it! He's won!'

Pulsating roars of exultation boomed around the room and Bernie was quick to seize the moment.

'Here he comes!'

With a barely containable look of elation filling his face, he bounded out with a youthful swagger, as though ready to break another junior mile record on the tracks of NYC.

By the time he reached the dais, the crowd had erupted into a heaving chant of,

'Bernie, Bernie, Bernie...'

The large gymnasium shook as the name of the victor reverberated in echoing delight off the walls. I've seen AC/DC in concert and even that paled in comparison to the energy emanating from this gathering.

I was weeping tears of full-bodied joy, while also slam-jump celebrating like a pogo stick on speed. This was the moment I'd dreamt of when embarking on my political odyssey.

Bernie tried to start his speech for what seemed like a good (actually, great) few minutes, but the overflowing commendations would not relent.

I love seeing it when Bernie gets coy; he's very cute for a guy closing in on 80. Having been overlooked for mass attention for most of his many years of dedicated public service, he never quite looks comfortable being a political idol to screaming fans.

He was blushing and stretching out his spindly arms to point at many of the faces he recognised in the gushing mob before him. These acknowledging gestures with his corresponding smiling nods of approbation showed that even in this 'yuge' moment of personal triumph, he was throwing the credit back to those who fought for him. You could sense him internally verbalising,

'You all made this possible!'

And

'I couldn't have done this without you!'

He also threw in a few little left-right air jab combos, to symbolise the ongoing fight, making him the world's oldest Rocky impersonator.

I thought for a second he might even launch himself into the throng, twisting mid-air, to be thrown around the room in a festive display of crowd-surfing jubilance. Sadly, no.

He spoke with passion, grace, and heart. We were in raptures. His family had joined him on stage, and I caught Raymond making eye contact with Bernie's son, Levi, who motioned back with direct acknowledgement. I glanced across at Raymond with a curious look,

'I was a database administrator for his campaign when he ran for Congress here in New Hampshire a couple of years back.'

'No shit! You're full of surprises, aren't you!'

249

I'd also heard in passing that Raymond worked with the 'Sanders for President' Reddit page, started in 2014, that is attributed as being a major force in building momentum for Bernie after he first announced his presidential run, and polls showed that 3% of the US population had ever heard of him. Raymond was a man of many talents and just hanging out with him as he livestreamed moments etc. made me pick up on the fact that he was super tech savvy. I learned he was a system and network engineer and had put those skills into practice for a range of progressive causes. A smart man with a good heart.

We piled back into town to Shoppers Pub, where I'd picked up my ticket for the Jeanne Shaheen dinner thingy at SNHU arena a few days earlier. It had been pumping for hours. The Chapo team was there as well as many campaign officials, including Shannon Jackson, the state director.

The campaign had opened up the bar for beers and pizza on Bernie. It seemed as though the early attendees had been taking full advantage of this. The main crew took turns jumping up on top of a central table and regaling the room with gratitude and targeted calls for significant staff to stand and drink as the rest of the team whooped and hollered appreciatively. Shannon Jackson gave sweeping thanks to all and was showered with praise, love, and beer.

Spilling out into the street, when finally told to move on by the bar staff, we mingled merrily out front.

'Ah, that's where the Seu-Neu-Hoo Arena is!', joked one girl as she saw the SNHU Arena with its large title-affirming sign looking down at us from across the road.

Actually, she declared this a few times, equally amused each time.

Raymond checked his phone,

'Ah, damn it! I missed a call from Levi!'

Bugger.

Would have been amazing to get a guernsey into the inner sanctum for celebrations. Imagine Nina and Cornel in beast mode behind closed doors. It wasn't to be, as it was now well past midnight, and I'd imagine Bernie wasn't in the middle of an all-night beer binge.

The time came to say goodbye,

'I'll be back for Bernie's inauguration. See you there.'

'Oooh, yeah! You'd better believe it.'

Big hugs were shared with special focus on farewells to Chris and Raymond, with whom I'd spent a large part of the last few days. Memories that will stand the test of time.

A like-minded international visitor, who was one of very few not drinking, offered to drop me back at Albert's. His overall mission wasn't quite as lengthy as mine, but his day's efforts were commendable. He'd driven down from Montreal to attend the results party and was about to set off to complete the return leg of his short-term migration until well into the night. He was a cracking lad who knew he had to be there to share in this memorable occasion.

I thanked him warmly, despite the temperature at this hour being well below freezing, and went up and through Albert's unlocked door to pass a fresh rotation of unfamiliar faces crashed out on couch and floor in this haven for Bernie's heroes. I snuck past into the room that I was sharing with young Simon, who had already nodded off on his portable mattress that he'd set up on the floor. Perhaps in deference to my age, I had been offered a single bed and, with the justification that it would help placate any awkward questioning from an inquisitive wife, accepted with fleeting hesitation and deliberately feeble attempts to decline the generous offer.

That night, for so many different reasons, I slept like a king.

K. It's a Big Club and You Ain't in it

George Carlin was one of the most prescient (and funny) observers of modern America:

> *YouTube: George Carlin It's a big club and you ain't in it*

'*But there's a reason. There's a reason. There's a reason for this, there's a reason education sucks, and it's the same reason that it will never, ever, ever be fixed. It's never gonna get any better. Don't look for it. Be happy with what you got.*

Because the owners of this country don't want that. I'm talking about the real owners now, the real owners, the big wealthy business interests that control things and make all the important decisions.

Forget the politicians. The politicians are put there to give you the idea that you have freedom of choice. You don't. You have no choice. You have owners. They own you. They own everything. They own all the important land. They own and control the corporations.

They've long since bought and paid for the senate, the congress, the state houses, the city halls, they got the judges in their back pockets and they own all the big media companies so they control just about all of the news and information you get to hear. They got you by the balls.

They spend billions of dollars every year lobbying, lobbying, to get what they want. Well, we know what they want. They want more for themselves and less for everybody else, but I'll tell you what they don't want: They don't want a population of citizens capable of critical thinking. They don't want well informed, well educated people capable of critical thinking. They're not interested in that. That doesn't help them. That's against their interests. That's right. They don't want people who are smart enough to sit around a kitchen table to figure out how badly they're getting fucked by a system that threw them overboard 30 fucking years ago. They don't want that.

You know what they want? They want obedient workers. Obedient workers. People who are just smart enough to run the machines and do the paperwork, and just dumb enough to passively accept all these increasingly shittier jobs with the lower pay, the longer hours, the reduced benefits, the end of overtime and the vanishing pension that disappears the minute you go to collect it, and now they're coming for your Social Security money. They want your retirement money.

They want it back so they can give it to their criminal friends on Wall Street, and you know something? They'll get it. They'll get it all from you, sooner or later, 'cause they own this fucking place.

It's a big club, and you ain't in it.

You and I are not in the big club. And by the way, it's the same big club they use to beat you over the head with all day long when they tell you what to believe. All day long beating you over the head in their media telling you what to believe, what to think and what to buy.

The table is tilted folks. The game is rigged, and nobody seems to notice, nobody seems to care. Good honest hard-working people — white collar, blue collar, it doesn't matter what colour shirt you have on — good honest hard-working people continue — these are people of modest means — continue to elect these rich cocksuckers who don't give

*a fuck about them. They don't give a fuck about you. They don't give
a fuck about you. They don't care about you at all — at all — at all.*

*And nobody seems to notice, nobody seems to care. That's what the
owners count on; the fact that Americans will probably remain will-
fully ignorant of the big red, white and blue dick that's being jammed
up their assholes everyday. Because the owners of this country know
the truth: it's called the American Dream, because you have to be asleep
to believe it.'*

RIP George.

*I used to play football (soccer) with a high-ranking member of
the US armed forces in Korea. During the heated run-in to the 2016
election, when Democrats and Republicans were at each other's throats
with scathing daily portrayals of the other side, he went back to the
States for a high-level meeting and he told me a brief anecdote from
that trip:*

*In a plush and pricey NY restaurant, he saw DWS (Debbie-Was-
serman Schultz), then head of the DNC, walk in and spy Ted Cruz,
the far-right punching bag for Dems and aligned media, on the far
side of the room. They greeted each other almost in the manner of that
fabled scene where lovers run across the fields in slow motion to embrace. Their extended chat was full of hugs, hearty laughter and blatant familiarity, friendship, and enjoyment. On TV, they hate each
other.*

It's all a game.

*The tightly controlled 2-party system sees the Dems and Repubs
sharing a grossly overlapping pool of donors (most big money interests
want a foot in both camps, so there is no losing outcome). Although, it is
generally agreed that the elephants have stronger ties with big oil and
gas companies, arms manufacturers, and real estate interests, whereas
the donkeys dominate health insurance, entertainment (Hollywood*

connections), and Silicon Valley Big Tech etc. This is where factional rivalries are at their fiercest; between people whose ride on the gravy train depends on who is wearing the driver's cap. Either way, though, the same train stays on the same track, just with a variation in the crew.

So, whilst the Repubs are clearly a grotesque menace to humanity, don't be confused into thinking that means the Dems are your friend.

The analogy Malcolm X used to describe racial attitudes is also suitable to summarise how the 2 major US parties treat the electorate,

'The white conservatives aren't friends of the Negro either, but they at least don't try to hide it. They are like wolves; they show their teeth in a snarl that keeps the Negro always aware of where he stands with them. But the white liberals are foxes, who also show their teeth to the Negro but pretend that they are smiling. The white liberals are more dangerous than the conservatives; they lure the Negro, and as the Negro runs from the growling wolf, he flees into the open jaws of the "smiling" fox. One is the wolf, the other is a fox. No matter what, they'll both eat you'.

I've heard the Democrats and Republicans described as two sides of the same coin. Gore Vidal observed in the 60s that they were becoming 'two wings of the same bird of prey'. I've even heard 'the twin heads of a corporate-funded snake'.

I'm gonna sugarcoat this a bit because I know people who may become sensitive about it. So I will start by pointing out that I believe Barack Obama to be the most gifted, charismatic performer that I have ever seen in the political realm. In terms of presentational politics, he is unparalleled. Stylistically peerless, so likeable, and very charming. But personality doesn't change people's lives, policies do. He made many people feel culturally superior to those nasty Republicans, but the substantive improvements to people's economic well-being were less forthcoming.

It is necessary to step out of Plato's cave in order to detach ourselves from corporate representations. By focusing on critical policy analysis alone, we can come to the clear realisation that neither major party has the people's interests prominently in mind, no matter how charmingly they pretend to.

Chomsky describes how mainstream messaging promotes vigorous debate within strictly limited boundaries of 'acceptable' options. Unless you are rich enough to be unconcerned by either elite-friendly option, the choice is terrible versus bad. Chomsky also explains how the left edge of this narrow, rightward drifting range, portrays itself to be so radically progressive that anything further left is seen as incomprehensible and dangerous. He explains how MSNBC and the NYT etc. are counterproductive to progressivism because they lull viewers/readers into thinking they are revolutionary fighters for justice when they are simply being corralled into the permissible corporate framework. The British duo of Davids, Cromwell and Edwards, who run the analysis website Media Lens, provide an outstanding elucidation of this (mainly in UK politics) in their book 'Propaganda Blitz'. It particularly highlights the role played by The Guardian and The BBC in hindering progressive hopes.

Chomsky no longer gets invited onto major US networks (last appearing in the 80s), but he is very active on independent media. One of his regular platforms is Democracy Now!, where many other leading lights in the world of political science academia can also be found - Naomi Klein, Joseph Stiglitz, Angela Davis, Arundhati Roy etc. These intellectuals have written extensively on the possibilities of making the world a better place and are very willing to share their research. If you haven't been tuned in to this information universe and have been getting most of your news from big networks and popular papers then my critique of Democratic Party leadership will no doubt strike you as surprising and maybe even shocking. But not if you've been regularly tapping into the greatest political science minds.

If you know someone better informed and more rational in their appraisal than Chomsky, let me know. For a little indication as to why he is no longer invited onto CNN and co., here he is in 2010 giving his views on the first couple of years of the Obama presidency along with a scarily prophetic prediction of what would follow,

---

YouTube: Chomsky on Liberal Disillusionment with Obama

Chomsky is not alone in these views. They are prevalent in the world of political science academia. I've been reading and watching these kinds of critiques for over a decade and they seem commonplace to me. These academic evaluations are not attached to allegiances to either party, but an overview of the system and the resultant policies entirely separated from image-based assessments and emotional affiliations.

I used to watch a lot of Jon Stewart's Daily Show and he also started calling Obama out early on. He expressed grave concerns when Obama, very soon after his inauguration, put Timothy Geithner in charge of the Treasury Dept. This former CEO of Goldman Sachs, which was at the heart of causing the devastating financial crisis, was now entrusted with leading the recovery program. It was like making Harvey Weinstein the head of an institute for victims of sexual abuse.

Obama also retained Bob Gates as Defense Secretary, much lauded as reaching across the aisle in a noble display of bi-partisan compromise. Bush's war guy. Are you fucking kidding?

Did the promised hope and change suddenly not include a much-vaunted change of tack in Iraq while also handing financial control to those who had just destroyed the US and world economy? Regular wanna-be homeowners had been screwed and were in desperate need of government support, but Goldman Sachs were put in charge instead.

I've heard all the reflexive apologies and conditioned justifications whenever suggesting that Obama doesn't shit pure gold. Any chance people were paying more attention to the slow jammin' the news, singing of Amazing Grace, mic drops, and those oh, so dramatic and powerful oratory pauses rather than examining the Wall St. hand-picked cabinet choices and policy enactments?

Goldman Sachs funded his campaign; it was now time for them to reap the benefits.

For the first 2 years of his reign, the Dems controlled all levers of government and had an overwhelming public mandate with sweeping support for Obama's platitudinal rhetoric of change. Where were the policy specifics, though?

Don't try to sell ObamaCare as one of his praise-worthy achievements, either. It is designed to maximise profits for the health insurance industry by mandating more people to pay higher prices. Also, the 30 million poorest Americans who need healthcare the most are left out. Why? Because they can't afford it and thus it isn't profitable. It's exactly the same system as RomneyCare (when Mitt was Governor of Massachusetts); both were drafted up by The Heritage Foundation, a right-wing thinktank, on behalf of medical insurance companies with money, not health, as their main agenda.

Some people hang on to their partisan devotion to Obamacare pretty tightly, even though the American healthcare system is cruel, dysfunctional, and very expensive - sometimes prohibitively so - directly costing lives. Remember that the US is the only developed nation not to have universal public healthcare.

The strongest emotional loyalty I've heard, comes from those who have not had first-hand experience of the soaring premiums, co-pays, and deductibles only to still get denied coverage due to a pre-existing condition (coverage is limited wherever possible to maximise profits). Having spoken with lots of Americans about this, it would seem that the image outperforms the reality. Compared to the Australian and Korean systems, it seems barbaric. Their system is the deceptively named Affordable Care Act, aka Obamacare. Unless you are rich, it sux. The Obama name attached to it nails down the brand allegiance, with some cognitive dissonance coming through as people passionately defend the worst healthcare system in the developed world – in the richest country in history, no less.

Only in a binary showdown against the right-wing's attempts to gut healthcare entirely and let the private health insurance industry run wild, is Obamacare preferable. In the same way that a punch in the gut is better than a punch in the head. By real-world metrics, it is terrible.

Using this same preferable punch analogy, progressives are standing outside the healthcare boxing ring with open arms offering a hug. We are branded radical lunatics for doing so. Despite committed efforts to misinform people, the Medicare-For-All 'hug' is also much cheaper and more efficient. Once you take out private medical insurance industry salaries (including bloated executive ones) along with the monstrous advertising and marketing costs, how could it not be?

Yet there is fear-mongering about how people will never accept this kind of 'socialist' agenda – the popular one used in every other democratic capitalist nation, that is. I'd be interested to see the actual electoral response when people see hundreds of dollars saved every month and are freely able to visit a doctor anytime. I want the

Republican party to be defeated so resoundingly that their reactionary agenda disappears into irrelevance. Implementing policies like Medi-care-For-All will ensure that this happens. People want help, and whoever gives it to them will be untouchable.

Political science academics have been on top of these realities for years – they don't subscribe to the 2-party ultimatum. The continuing 'hug' analogy, outside of the narrow duopolitical framing, also applies to a range of issues from climate change and military interventionism to racial justice, job programs, education, housing etc. The progressive options are the most popular when surveyed issue by issue, but neither party seems to put these choices on the table. Bernie has been trying for years to cut through the partisan bullshit to fight for what's right.

The Obama administration did, however, bring about the ground-breaking achievements of ushering in federal same-sex marriage laws and the important Iran Deal.

Who was paying sufficient attention to all the broken promises and public betrayals, though? Troop surges in Iraq and Afghanistan (war is cool when Dems do it), record deportations of immigrants, Or-wellian increases in public surveillance, Guantanamo Bay remaining open, authoritarian state crackdowns of whistleblower's civil liberties, ramped up militarisation of police departments, pushing through oil pipelines against indigenous land rights protests, advocating for cor-porate-written trade deals that would sell out both the working class and the environment. The list goes on.

At least Obama set a far calmer tone and engaged in none of the divisive rhetoric of the current fearmongerer-in-chief.

However, and I know this may be a bitter pill for some to swallow, to enact anything close to substantive, people-centred change, it's nec-essary to detach ourselves from any emotional allegiance or swooning belief that the corporate Dems are genuinely on the side of regular people, regardless of how stylishly they pretend to be.

I form my opinions of politicians based on their policy platforms and voting records. Talk is cheap, corporate lobbyist vote-buying is expensive. However, as an homage to evocative media paradigms, I'm gonna give 2 examples of visceral moments that left lasting impressions on my feelings toward Obama. People find it easier to shrug off or justify rational arguments; emotional impact is tougher to shirk.

After his resounding victory in 2008, the people of Flint, Michigan, especially the majority-minority of African-Americans had heart-lifting hope that their poisoned water problem would be fixed. The black knight in shining armor finally heeded the call and flew in for what appeared to be a rescue mission for the city in distress.

In a gob-smacking display of bad acting, though, mid-way through his press conference, Barry fake-sipped some local water with it barely, if at all, touching his lips and instantly proclaimed it to be fine. He then repeated this sickening (although he didn't actually drink it, so not literally) stunt for the cameras a short time later with the heinous Republican Governor, Rick Snyder, approvingly gawking on at close range.

This was the shattering of the last of any illusion that he might be on the side of the people. Astute political judges refer to this as the moment that sowed the seeds for Michigan to move over to Trump in 2016. The thing that surprises me most about this is whose idiotic call was it? Just stay away if that was gonna be your game. I thought his team were far slicker than that. Surely Obama was sharp enough to realise he should override such lunacy. Or were bigger factors at play and calling the shots? Follow the money. Have a look at Michael

Moore's 'Fahrenheit 11/9' (2019) to see this incident in all its disheartening detail.

I also followed the Colin Kaepernick kneeling for the anthem drama very closely back in 2016. A brave and principled use of his 1ˢᵗ Amendment rights for free speech, valiantly utilised to bring desperately-needed attention to the plight of black men being systemically brutalised and killed by police in disgracefully disproportionate numbers.

What a hero!

Or an anthem-disrespecting, flag-betraying, troop-hating national traitor. Shut up and play (sing/dance)! You are the entertainment; you're not allowed to use your media exposure for ethical good that challenges the money machine.

The super-rich, white old men that control the NFL, here a metaphor for the world, wouldn't stand for it, ironically. They unfurled tirades of abuse towards Kaepernick and blacklisted (appropriate term) him to ensure he wouldn't play again. The media almost universally fell in line, too.

How about big, bad Barry boy with the largest bully pulpit in the world? It was a chance to honour the record-breaking African-American support that raised him into this historic position that enabled him to affect change and bring positive reforms to the cruel, racist system which pervades US society.

I remember standing up with a clenched fist and taking a few deep breaths to avoid punching my computer monitor when Obama, asked about this on CNN, echoed mainstream concerns about dishonouring anthems, flags, and troops then wrapped it all in standard non-committal equivocations. Made my blood boil.

The comedian Patton Oswalt has a bit that he did in his Netflix stand-up special, 'Talking for Clapping', just before the November 2016 showdown,

'Look, I wanna woman president. I wanna gay president, alright. But just know that... Ok, hang on. I don't wanna be one of those guys that's like,

> 'Hey, man, there's people that actually are behind the president that run the country, man.'

But there are people behind the president that actually run the country. And it seems especially ever since Clinton, doesn't it feel like they've been casting the presidency to deliver something awful as a giant sugar... Like with Clinton it was,

> 'We've got this NAFTA thing and it fucks over the American workers and it destroys the manufacturing... How are we gonna sell this? Ok, here's what we do. We get a fun, kind of Southern Elvis-y dude. And he likes cheeseburgers and blowjobs. People will be like, 'Oh, that's kinda cool'.

And it worked! It worked. But then...

> 'Oh, now we got this torture...Oh, my God, this torture program's a nightmare. How in the hell are we gonna sell this? 'Oh, well, I know. We'll get a fun, bumbling cowboy. And he can't really talk, and he walks into doors. And he's fun. People will like that. And we'll get that through. Nice'.

'I don't know how else to put this. Flying assassin droids. We have flying assassin droids'.

> 'Cool black guy. I don't know another way...' 'I, uh... That's the first thing I thought. A cool black guy. There's no other way'.

So, look, again, I want a woman president, I want a gay president. I'm just letting you know, when we get those, there will be something horrible attached to them. By the time we get to gay president, that means we've got Soylent Green. That means we are putting people *in a giant mulcher and just making energy bars out of 'em. We gotta fucking… We gotta start eating people to survive.*

Get the funny gay guy out there, just…

'Whose hungry?' Like I…

'He's funny. I like him. It's cool. He's good. I like that guy.'

8.

New Hampshire Primary Day plus 1: Belting Down a Highway Untethered on a Mattress

Simon was a sweet kid from Nebraska, who'd retro-fitted his car into a mobile home so he could follow the Bernie campaign around the country on the cheap. He was softly spoken and had a heart of gold. I was glad he was sharing a room with me at Albert's, as it wasn't the kind of weather to be car-bound in overnight.

His mattress had been filling the entire interior of his car, other than the 2 front seats. However, he'd dragged it up into Albert's place, so he could still have a padded sleep after graciously relinquishing Albert's spare single bed to me.

New Hampshire was done; in the bag for Bernie. The support crew was breaking up and going in different directions. The main Bernie band; high-ranking campaign officials and super-committed volunteers, were straight on to Nevada then South Carolina. I would have loved to have stayed on tour, but was so happy to have done my little bit to help build some early momentum for team Bernie. I now needed to move on.

I'd booked a flight out of Boston in a few days, but first I was gonna kick back for a few relaxing days with my boss and great friend (same guy, which not too many can say), Barney, who was home visiting his delightful mum, Carolyn, in Connecticut.

Ted had arranged a lift for himself back to New York with the North-East regional director of the Democratic Socialists of America. He then teed up a seat for me, too, to be dropped off along the way. They were both staying about 20k (13m) south of Manchester, and I'd agreed to get to a designated pick-up point for a morning rendezvous. I was sweet to Uber down, but Simon said he was happy to drop me there, if I could wake him up.

That ended up being more difficult than it sounded, but I made him a cup of coffee and we were up and ready. Albert was dressed up and on his way to work. Right, I'd forgotten about stuff like that. I didn't even realise that he'd been working a regular Mon to Fri job (something in IT), while dedicating his every free hour to the campaign.

He'd stocked his kitchen with all sorts of goodies for his guests, like a generous guesthouse host, which he basically was. There were cereals, yoghurts, muffins, pastries, and energy bars galore. When we said we had to dash off, he insisted that we take provisions for the trip, but I thanked him again and assured him we'd stop off and get some food down the road. I passed on my genuine appreciation as he headed off to his office.

I then helped Simon lug his mattress back down to his car. He had a large cooler box strapped into his passenger seat, so he offered me the luxury recline mode of the back mattress for our short trip. I had the pleasure of being ferried around like a modern-day emperor, as I lay comfortably on the mobile mattress. I felt like I should've been in a toga being fed grapes.

I used my newfound delusions of imperial grandeur to remind my courteous courier to navigate the slippery streets with caution to avoid my sedan chair being refashioned into more of a flying carpet. He obliged - going through the quiet Manchester streets at a leisurely pace. I was feeling good after a smooth night's rest and a few minutes of bonus down time in transit.

Once on the freeway, though, I was a little more alert, as he needed to get up to a similar speed to the cars and trucks hurtling along either side of us. Any sudden loss of speed would have found me launched skywards into the surrounding New England forest with a front windshield for company.

It was now that Barney called me and I explained that I was reliving my university life by recklessly belting down a highway untethered on a mattress. Simon had it all under control, though, and we got into the pre-arranged café meet zone with enough time for me to treat us both to a hearty breakfast, as promised.

Team Ted turned up on time, I gave Simon a big hug, waved farewell to the mattress-mobile, and we set sail southward out of New Hampshire.

We had a quick detour to pick up a friend of the driver in a rich, semi-rural community where people owned stables on large tracts of land, before getting back onto the interstate and zipping along again.

Barney is from Waterford, Connecticut, which was a decent diversion from the fastest route to NY. I happily agreed to be dropped at the train station in New Haven for a short coastal jaunt eastward along Long Island Sound to my destination. Ted liked the sound of some train travel, too, and decided to jump off at the same station to avoid the Manhattan traffic and deposit himself back into the heart of world business by Amtrak.

We were heading in different directions, as my trip was 40 minutes back along the Connecticut coast, which the freeway had overshot. I had about 20 minutes to kill and Ted a bit longer. We grabbed a quick snack, and a final coffee. I was cutting it a bit fine when making a move, so when I began my heartfelt farewell,

'It's been a real pleasure to spend some time with you...'

Ted interjected. New York style.

'Yup! I've got your details. You'd better get going.'

It was a pleasant ride with ocean views the whole way and my mate was there to greet me. I spent the next few days unwinding with Barney and his lovely mum. Home-cooked meals – roast chicken, clam chowder. Days filled with coastal walks, trips to bookstores and bike shops. I was wonderfully well looked after, and this all seemed like a true taste of life in the small-town American dream.

Feeling relaxed and refreshed, I jumped on a train to brutally cold Boston, where my 2 weeks came to a close.

A fortnight at Bernie's.

L. The Arc of the Moral Universe is Long, but it Bends Towards Justice

After the US, I went down to Oz to spend time with family and friends (my wife joined me) before resuming my university teaching semester in Seoul in March. My Aussie sojourn was granted a corona-extension, as the start of my uni year was delayed, so I was still down there as Super Tuesday came and went, along with Bernie's chances.

Bernie had won the popular vote in the first 3 primaries; a position from which no previous candidate had failed to secure the nomination (actually, no-one had previously lost after winning the first 2). But the undeniable power of the media never rallied around this fact, instead heaping equivocations and negative narratives on Bernie's successes (including his resounding support from the Latino community in Nevada). However, after floundering in the first 3 states (finishing 4th, 5th, and 2nd), after 1 victory in South Carolina, Biden was suddenly anointed as the presumptive nominee.

The electability narrative had been very successfully hijacked, combined with the masterful last-minute pre-Super Tuesday alignment of powerful political and media forces for Biden. Many traditional voters were blindsided into falling in line after the 11th hour drop-outs/endorsements from Buttigieg and Klobuchar (and Warren's abandoning of progressive chances by vainly pushing on), along with co-ordinated post-South Carolina pro-Biden media chest-beating.

This Obama-prompted establishment coalescing around Biden proved to be a brilliantly effective transformation of the primary calculus, providing Uncle Joe with a sudden surge of endorsed momentum. This confirmed that it had always been Bernie against the rest as the consolidation of the full range of institutional advantages across America's entrenched political and media landscape were unleashed to their full potential. Big Media showed that they still had enough muscle to overwhelmingly push consent for Biden into the lead narrative. It was a powerful flex. (This corporate consent-forming stranglehold will continue to weaken, however, as demographics turn – fewer and fewer people under 50 regularly tune in to cable news or routinely read mainstream newspapers).

They all then triumphantly circled the wagons around Biden, leaving Bernie's campaign vulnerable. He fought on for a bit, but was exposed to mainstream attacks and painfully bent the knee after hacks had aggressively called for it, but before it was necessary, in my opinion.

It was over.

People kept asking me,

> *'How do you feel about Bernie being out?'*

> > *'Disappointed,' was the understatement I would come up with.*

> > *'Oh, well…,' was the common flippant, half-arsed sympathy offered, as people dismissed it from their mind.*

Some even enquired,

> *'You went over there, didn't you?'*

> > *'Yeah.'*

'It's a long way to go. How was it?'

'Good.'

I didn't know how to summarise my thoughts into a digestible response, so one word was often all I could come up with.

Most of those asking this were family or close friends. I'd spoken to some of them about my crusading beliefs before, but I felt that my reticence now wasn't doing myself justice. I felt compelled to put something down on paper to keep a record of my experiences and feelings, and to help me find some peace of mind and soothe my aching soul. It was so cathartic, I couldn't stop. It felt like therapy for a broken heart.

There is a deeply complicated word in Korean, 'han', which I couldn't do justice to fully comprehending or adequately explaining, but it represents a complex entwining of emotions such as sorrow, regret, resentment, and deep-seated angst, all underpinned by an idealistic hope that things will get better. According to Wikipedia,

'The minjung theologian Suh Nam-dong describes han as "a feeling of unresolved resentment against injustices suffered, a sense of helplessness because of the overwhelming odds against one, a feeling of acute pain in one's guts and bowels, making the whole body writhe and squirm, and an obstinate urge to take revenge and to right the wrong—all these combined".'

It continues, saying that in the West Wing episode using this Korean concept as its title,

'In "Han", Josiah Bartlet, the president of the United States, says, "There's a Korean word, Han. I looked it up. There is no literal English translation. It's a state of mind. Of soul, really. A sadness. A sadness so deep no tears will come. And yet, still, there's hope."'

So, if I had to sum up my feelings in one word, it would be this Korean word, 'han'.

It is now August (2020) as I wrap up my writing, and the world has obviously been knocked off its feet by coronavirus, along with the horrendous murder of George Floyd leading to fully-justified global protests breaking out against racial injustice. Add to this the increasing economic hardships piled onto people in nations where the government has failed to provide adequate pandemic support to its citizens and, amidst all this, climate catastrophe still looms as undoubtedly the greatest threat facing humanity. Dark times.

In the US, Trump continues to expose himself as a narcissistic sociopath, devoid of any empathy towards others. His dedication to his own fragile ego and the evil interests of himself and his co-conspirators against all that is kind and humane, has become criminally glaring. His shallow, self-centred incompetence has led directly to the unnecessary loss of a massive number of lives, in order to serve the needs of those controlling the top-end economic profits. Just evil.

With the opportunity for Bernie to provide the antithetical counterpoint to this with a moral, expert-driven, non-corporate-compromised set of solutions now lost, we are stuck with Biden.

Having been intimately involved in the first couple of weeks of the primary, this seems absurd. It is the upside down.

There is absolutely no doubt, however, that the menace and destruction being caused by the Trump regime must be brought to a halt. Things are spiralling out of control with dangerous potential of increased authoritarian measures being put in place. It is time to vote these wanna-be despots out on their arse and to usher in a new administration.

This does not make me a big fan of Biden, though. He has been at the coalface of every neo-liberal decision (vote) that has led us down the errant path to where we are today. Biden was the architect of the 1994 crime bill (3 strikes and you're out & mandatory minimum

sentencing even for non-violent crimes) leading to mass incarcera-
tion on behalf of the for-profit private prison industry. He backed
every trade bill (NAFTA, U.S.–China Relations Act of 2000, etc.)
that offshored US manufacturing jobs and gutted the industrial
Mid-West. He helped write the Patriot Act (2001), the G.W. Bush-
era crackdown on civil liberties. He voted for the Iraq War (2002)
and for repealing the Glass-Steagall financial regulations (1999),
leading directly to the Global Financial Crisis in 2007/8. And the
list goes on and on.

However, with massive caveats, I'm actually warming to the idea
of Biden in the Oval Office, ironically because he would be such a
piss-weak president. If he gets to sit in the big chair (the throne of the
US empire), he will have the weakest, almost non-existent, mandate.
Yes, he needs to stem the haemorrhaging damage of the Trump regime.
But, what else?

Obama entered office with a sweeping mandate from the people,
who disengaged in the expectation that Barry would take care of im-
plementing his vague promises. Currently, there is energy in the streets
at a level unprecedented since the 60s with today's activism coming
from the younger half of the population, who have had enough and are
now prepared to stand up for a safer, healthier future. These people are
not gonna readily sit down for bumbling Uncle Joe.

He needs to be forced into enacting policies to repair the US's sys-
temic faults, which have become far worse over the last 40+ years and
are tearing the nation apart. Public pressure must bring about major
reforms to address the rampant wealth inequality, racial injustices,
environmental disregard, and military destruction that have dimin-
ished America's status in the world and tarnished its soul.

Biden's successful presidential campaign strategy so far has been to
lie very low; advisable in the age of COVID-19 and when you also

*put your foot in your mouth almost every time you open it. He has,
however, remained consistent with his policy commitments of,*

> *'I'm not Trump.'*

And

> *'Aww, c'mon man. You've got to be kidding me. No, I'm seri-
ous. This is just a bunch of malarkey.'*

*(showing off his working-class schtick that continues to deceive
people into thinking that 'regular Joe' is on their side; not a stooge put
in place in the 70s to establish and protect the credit card industry's
corporate tax loophole in Delaware).*

*Ludicrously, these will hopefully be enough. It would be superb to
see the Donald implode in a resounding banishment to the dustbin of
history with the Dems ending up with control of both houses and the
White House. We could discard the myopic lens focused on comparing
everything to Trump. Then pressure could be applied to actually enact
policies to help people. No excuses.*

*I understand the reservations felt by progressives who consider this
approach foolhardy, as it had fallen flat before. But I want to believe
that things are different this time – the awareness and energy ready to
push for progressive change are desperate to be unleashed.*

*Along with concerted public pressure and directed campaigns to
influence elected representatives, the more progressives that make it
to DC to join AOC and the squad (Ilhan Omar, Rashida Tlaib, and
Ayanna Pressley) the better.*

*Possibly the most important speech Bernie has even given was
shortly after he dropped out of the running in 2016. He put forward
a rousing argument that he couldn't bring about ethical reforms alone,
and he called out for as many people as possible to sign up to run for office
(or to nominate someone who you think would be suitable) at all levels
'from local dog catcher up to Congress and everything in-between', to*

paraphrase the great man. People responded in droves (over 15,000 names were registered in the first few days). It was then that progressive organisations were formed to interview, train, and promote these new 'people's candidates'. Our Revolution was immediately set up by Bernie staffers, along with Justice Democrats, Brand New Congress, and others. This hard work is now starting to bear fruit. And it is still early in the growth of this large progressive orchard.

This is just the beginning.

Jamaal Bowman, Mondaire Jones, Marie Newman, Cori Bush, and other true progressives are in with an extremely positive chance of joining the squad in Congress after November and bringing a brighter spotlight to issues in the public's interest.

These representatives will spearhead the fight for Medicare-for-all, the Green New Deal, an overhaul of policing and criminal justice systems, a federal jobs guarantee (or UBI), and housing protections, etc. All of these were Bernie's policies that were described as radical and fanciful just 6 months ago. Reality is now proving these things to not only be possible, but essential.

With concerted top and bottom pressure, the progressive movement will continue to build momentum, meaning that a better future is definitely possible. I believe that many other people are coming to this same realisation.

Busted up for a couple of months after Bernie's butchering, progressives have dusted ourselves off and are back up fighting fit.

We cannot let up now. We know what needs to be done.

I will be back in the US before too long (all things being equal) to continue the battle.

If not beforehand, you would seriously struggle to stop me from getting stuck right into the thick of the action for AOC and/or Nina 2024.

Bring it on!

As I said many times to the multitude of phenomenal friends that I made on this incredibly inspiring journey (all of whom I hope to join forces with again),

'Keep fighting the good fight!'

Made in the USA
Middletown, DE
11 November 2021

51449631R00170